AF365529

WORLDING LOVE, GENDER, AND CARE

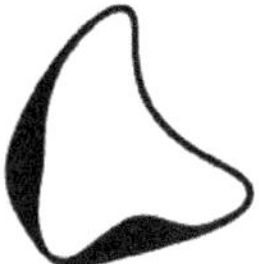

Worlding Public Cultures

This publication series investigates the global dimensions of contemporary public culture through the concept of 'worlding', an understanding of the world generated through continuous processes of world-making. The deployment of 'worlding' in this series builds on the postcolonial project of critiquing universalized Eurocentric frameworks, and is committed to a radical ontology of relationality. Going beyond current top-down models of inclusion, diversity, and other representations of the global, the series critiques radical alterity in favour of a pluriversality attendant to entanglements, difficult histories, and power relations. It grounds the global within local and transculturally/transnationally intertwined worlds, and foregrounds the possibility of continuously making and re-making new worlds through the arts.

WORLDING LOVE, GENDER, AND CARE
Shigeko Kubota's *Sexual Healing*

FRANZISKA KOCH

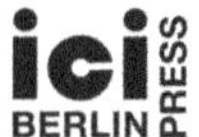

ISBN (Print): 978-3-96558-060-2
ISBN (PDF): 978-3-96558-061-9
ISBN (EPUB): 978-3-96558-062-6

Worlding Public Cultures
ISSN (Print): 2939-9211
ISSN (Online): 2939-922X

Bibliographical Information of the German National Library
The German National Library lists this publication in the Deutsche
Nationalbibliografie (German National Bibliography); detailed
bibliographic information is available online at http://dnb.d-nb.de.

© 2023 ICI Berlin Press

Cover design: Studio Bens
Cover image: Video still of Shigeko Kubota's *Sexual Healing* (1998),
courtesy of the Estate of Shigeko Kubota. Full credit on p. 31.

Except for images or otherwise noted, this publication is licensed under a
Creative Commons Attribution-ShareAlike 4.0 International License.
To view a copy of this license, visit:
http://creativecommons.org/licenses/by-sa/4.0/.
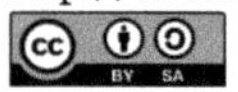

In Europe, the print edition is printed by Lightning Source UK Ltd., Milton
Keynes, UK. See the final page for further details.

The digital edition can be downloaded freely at:
https://doi.org/10.37050/wpc-ca-02.

ICI Berlin Press is an imprint of
ICI gemeinnütziges Institut für Cultural Inquiry Berlin GmbH
Christinenstr. 18/19, Haus 8
D-10119 Berlin
publishing@ici-berlin.org
press.ici-berlin.org

For Monica

Contents

We lived in a community. Fluxus is
sharing […]. All artists have ego,
but how you share ego together
with one goal — that's Fluxus.[1]

Shigeko Kubota

My first viewing of the short video *Sexual Healing* (1998), by the pioneering Japanese multimedia artist Shigeko Kubota (1937–2015), took place while I was researching artistic collaborations in the context of Fluxus in New York via the Electronic Arts Intermix archive.[2] I remember how the work felt more like shock therapy than a teasing cure. I was faced with the unexpected sight of the global shooting star of new media art, Nam June Paik (1932–2006), as a visibly aged and semi-paralysed patient struggling with simple movements such as standing up and walking. Despite being well acquainted with radical Fluxus humour and the groundbreaking experimental video work of both Paik and Kubota, it was hard to embrace the video's use of shrill contrast. While the eponymous pop song's lyrics stereotypically fantasize about a female nurse as sexually effective 'medicine' for the lovesick male singer, the music guides the rapid and repetitive cuts of a filmed reality, the original sounds of which are muted. However, it seems to scream loudly about the physically demanding, utterly non-erotic labour of several real nurses trying to get the disabled artist back on his feet. I do not recall whether the apparent contradiction lured me at first into a puzzled smile. However, every time I have viewed the video since, the recurring key scenes in which Paik abruptly and unsolicitedly kisses one or another of his caretakers, make me pause. They choke any good-humoured attempt to read the work as simply denoting a mocking homage by Kubota to her husband Paik in old age.

Rather, the video puts pressure on the epistemological boundaries of Art History, which have shaped its archives and canons according to gendered, cultural, and institutional hierarchies. Representing the little-explored nexus between love, sex, and care in old age, the video echoes the much-debated field of Fluxus collaborations, particularly its attack on singular (white, male, genius) authorship and its ideal of working together equally when fusing life and art. In particular, the work complicates existing views on the vital contribution of female Fluxus artists and shows how Kubota ambivalently projects her take on the world, love, and care in relation to gender issues.

Kubota and Paik's time together spanned over four decades. After initial brief moments of contact in Japan in 1963/64, later in 1964 they started participating in Fluxus activities in New York, which is where their initial romantic relationship began, leading to their marriage much later in 1977.[3] Following Paik's stroke in 1996, the couple increasingly shuttled between New York and Miami until his death in 2006, followed nine years later by Kubota's. Yet Kubota was notably clear in an interview with the curator Miwako Tezuka in 2009 that she did not see herself as Paik's artistic 'partner', but rather as 'his comrade'. She noted, '*I never collaborated with him.* We are very different, like water and oil.'[4] While this statement is substantiated by the fact that the couple co-authored only two video works,[5] there is broad visual and material evidence that they shared a vital interest in particular themes, engaged in similar aesthetics, used the same media technology (video, video sculptures, the Paik-Abe-video synthesizer), and greatly benefitted from each other's technological and compositional inventions.[6]

Rather than uncritically agreeing with Kubota, I will revisit moments of their collaboration and several earlier works that already negotiated sex and gender, before turning to *Sexual Healing* as a case study for discussing Kubota's 'worlding' of love, gender, and care. My question is what can one learn when taking into account the highly personal, embarrassing, encroaching, but also the ironic, touching, and caring aspects of *Sexual Healing*. How can we 'cure' Art History's institutional and methodological afflictions of modern Eurocentrism, patriarchal structures, and colonial legacies — such that it allows us to discern 'textures of affect and [...] different modes of knowledge beyond that of our scholarship — the artistic, the everyday and non-professional'[7] to write (global) art history in more personal, intimately situated, decolonial, and transcultural ways?[8]

After revisiting Kubota's pioneering first and only performance, *Vagina Painting* (1965), in the context of Paik's earlier attempt to shatter musical conventions by fusing it with open displays of (female) nudity in *Opera Sextro-*

nique (1964), her late work can be understood as a self-empowering return to the issues of love, care, and intimacy. *Sexual Healing* foregrounds Kubota's role in 'taking care' of her partner as well as her assumption of artistic authority as she ambivalently presents Paik's disability and inappropriate behaviour towards his caretakers. Beyond the ethics of representing care that the work raises, I also argue here that the video suggests a 'cure' to the kind of gendered realities of caretaking on the one hand, and patriarchal structures determining the canonization of video artists on the other. In doing so, it presents both a 'worlded' and 'worlding' feminist approach to the fraught issues of power undermining conventional concepts of female love and care, charging them with strong and ambivalent affect.[9] These haunt the viewer to the extent of jeopardizing a smooth public and institutional reception of the work, evident in the infrequent screenings and lack of scholarly attention the video has received so far.[10] The ethical discomfort we experience when viewing Kubota's late work arguably underscores an aesthetic regime that still favours the image of the singular genius artist (male or female) obscuring complex collaboration and dismissing works that challenge established societal norms that frame our gaze and worldviews. It questions art historical knowledge production, juxtaposing it with conflicted affect and gendered subjectivity, which invites us to ponder ways of knowing 'otherwise'.

THE WORLDING POWER OF AFFECT — AN IMPEDIMENT TO ART HISTORICAL RECEPTION?

Critical discussions in comparative and world literature studies,[11] popular culture studies,[12] theoretical reflections across feminism and physics,[13] anthropology,[14] and art history[15] have suggested 'world-making' and 'worlding' as a situated, relational, and planetary concept. 'Worlding' is a critical practice used to grapple with the complexities of globalization and transnationalism by acknowledging the problematic limits and impacts of modern Eurocentric epistemologies that have informed artistic practice as well as scholarly discourse worldwide following imperial and colonial expansions. As Birgit Mara Kaiser — building on Karen Barad's concept of 'intra-action' — has aptly summarized, the dynamic and procedural understanding of 'worlding' postulates world-wide and entangled artistic knowledge production as part of an 'intensified intra-action and a perpetually differentiating "world" — "world" as continuously in the making'.[16] This includes an understanding of culture as always already informed by transculturation, not uncritically subscribing to the modern nation-centred concept of cultures as homogenous containers that then interact and eventually hybridize.[17] Rather, 'culture' as well as 'world' are not static and given, waiting for an external subject to reflect and behold them, but their 'differential relational emergence means that beings (bodies, texts, cultures, nations [and I would like to add: images]) are considered in "their differential becoming, [as] particular material (re-)configurations of the world with shifting boundaries and properties that stabilize and destabilize".[18] Methodologically, the challenge then lies in situating the dynamic ways in which artists 'world', since their and our positionalities define what we see and mean when speaking about the 'world'. The inseparable ethical task is to acknowledge how we as scholars are implicated as well as indebted, and consciously relate to these worlds and worldings, ultimately questioning the dichotomy between knowing and being that has been one of the most prominent tenets of Art History's (modern) formation.

In what follows, I look to Kubota's *Sexual Healing* as a prism which highlights that ambivalent affect is a strong force of world-making that tends to be ignored or disqualified as being too personal, mundane, and messy to be allowed to have an impact on art historical canonization. I will argue that while conventionally object-centred art historical analysis often acknowledges the capacity of art works to generate affect, the artists' affect tends to be treated as an ambivalent challenge best relegated to peripheral biographical or ancillary psychological contextualization. In particular, when artists overtly express strong, negative, or even violent emotions in connection with love, grief, jealousy, anger, antipathy, or hate, it questions social and gendered norms of how such affect should be expressed and aesthetically resolved. However, if we attempt to open up conventional art historiography and question its epistemological conditions to make it a more diverse, inclusive, and even pluriversal undertaking, we have to account for complex affect and its 'worlding' power.[19]

SHIGEKO KUBOTA: EARLY PRACTICE AND PERSONAL LIFE

Born into a Buddhist family in Niigata, Japan, in 1937, Shigeko Kubota earned a degree in sculpture in 1960 from Tokyo University of Education. In her first solo exhibition, organized in the pioneering Naiqua Gallery in December 1963,[20] she engaged with issues of love and gender.[21] She provocatively called the show '1st Love, 2nd Love…' and 'piled up fragments of love letters from the floor up to the ceiling of the gallery',[22] covered with a white cloth, inviting visitors to climb on the mound-like environment. The precarious arrangement yielded half-hidden welded metal sculptures, some phallic or breast-like in shape with dangerously sharp edges, provoking ambiguous rather than romantic images of love, and intimate relations as transient and sometimes wounding encounters.[23] At the time, the artist was part of a densely interwoven and internationally well-informed network of postwar action artists, musicians, and performance artists pursuing anti-art, non-art, and neo-Dadaist ideas in Tokyo and beyond.[24] Kubota's decision to emigrate was influenced by the American composer John Cage, specifically by his concerts in Tokyo with the pianist David Tudor in 1962,[25] as well as the Korean Nam June Paik staging Fluxus scores in Sōgetsu Hall on 29 May 1964,[26] and befriending female role models such as the Japanese artist Yoko Ono,[27] who described the Tokyo art scene to the 'chairman of Fluxus', the Lithuanian George Maciunas. More importantly, Japan's conservative values at the time did not suit her experimental interests.[28] Armed with a letter of invitation from Maciunas, Kubota successfully applied for a visa and landed in New York on 4 July 1964, becoming the 'vice-president of Fluxus' shortly after her arrival.[29]

Reflecting on the aesthetic and material dimensions of Kubota's early works, Midori Yoshimoto has demonstrated the crucial role played by the trope of a potentially aching romantic love juxtaposed with a focus on experimental explorations of the (female) body. It also partially informs the artist's later series of video films, generally referred to as her 'video diary'. While the first Fluxus performance she realized in New York was belatedly but rightly canonized as a fundamental contribution to feminism in art, its relation to similar practices by Paik has not been thoroughly explored. Although linking it to his oeuvre risks undermining the successful feminist recuperation of Kubota's *Vagina Painting*, I argue that considering Paik's previous performances and their relationship as an important backdrop to the work does not necessarily diminish the performance's pioneering value. Rather, it serves to provide a more complex understanding of the gender and collaborative issues at stake in early Fluxus practices, as well as highlighting how the interpersonal relations with Paik shaped Kubota's practice as an act of 'worlding' contemporary art through a gendered and transcultural lens.

OPERA SEXTRONIQUE (1965)

To understand the role and relevance of aesthetic authority, artistic authorship, and the collaborative aspects of this performance, it helps to revisit Paik's earlier uses of nudity. At the beginning of the 1960s, while promoting the emergent Fluxus scene in the German Rheinland, Paik developed the idea of fusing sex and music as part of his *Aktionsmusik* ('action music'), demanding:

> After the liberation of music of the 20th century in three regards (serial — indeterminist — actionist) ... I have found out that we have to get rid of yet another chain ... which is ... PRE-FREUDIAN HYPOCRISY. Why is sex, a predominant theme in arts and literature, a taboo only in music? How long can New Music afford to lag behind our times by 60 years and still claim to be serious art? It is exactly the purification of sex under the pretext of being 'serious' that undermines the so-called 'seriousness' of music as classical art compared with literature and painting. Music needs its D. H. Lawrence, its Sigmund Freud.[30]

Paik's argument points to the fact that the music interpreter's body is conventionally asked to refrain from any other expression than that of virtuously creating the appropriate sounds. In contrast, he dreamt of music that would fuse body and mind, directly relating the somatic with auditory experiences, ultimately transgressing the demarcations of established art forms and the division of sensory perception. As art historian Joan Rothfuss has shown, Paik even imagined a kind of visceral climax produced by tuning the interior of the female body and transforming her into a quintessential instrument. According to Rothfuss, Paik referred to the 'ocular harpsichord' imagined by Louis Bertrand Castel, an eighteenth-century Jesuit monk:

> Castel's plan described a keyboard linked to panes of colored glass that were illuminated by candlelight when a key was struck. Paik quipped that his innovation in *Opera Sextronique* 'was to make a color organ with nude lady's organ itself!! Can you imagine [a] more consequent combination? And how many colors and keys have our woman's eternal organ!!!'[31]

In reality, Paik's radically objectifying fantasy of directly playing a woman through her internal organs was unattainable. Professional sex workers declined to perform a striptease as part of his *Etude for Pianoforte,* so he resolved to strip down to his underpants when performing *Sonata quasi una Fantasia* in the 1962 'Neo-Dada in der Musik' festival in Düsseldorf.[32]

As Martha Rosler has critically observed, 'the thread of [Paik's] work includes the fetishization of a female body as an instrument that plays itself, and the complementary thread of homage to other famous male artist-magicians or seers (quintessentially, [John] Cage)',[33] and while Paik's emphasis on the female body was not exclusive, he clearly did not undermine prevailing gender norms and iconic stereotypes when questioning musical conventions by confronting them with female nudity. Paik's original idea of using a female body would almost certainly have been scuppered by women's resistance to providing a body to fetishize — had it not been for the classically trained American cellist Charlotte Moorman in 1964.[34] Together, they embarked on a long-term collaboration that included the infamous *Opera Sextronique*, in which Moorman played the cello in several stages of undress. In contrast to an earlier rendition staged in Paris in 1965, Moorman was arrested when performing it on 9 February 1967 in New York's Judson Hall and convicted of obscenity, violating communal laws of decency, and having performed a piece that was 'utterly without social importance'.[35] Broad news coverage made their collaboration famous while also branding her with the epithet of 'topless cellist' for the rest of her life, albeit not always to her detriment.[36] Laura Wertheim Joseph has analysed the 'strategic possibilities of Moorman's refusal to resolve the tension between decisive artist and manipulated object', and convincingly concluded that:

> Moorman hovers between two equally credible personas: that of the virtuoso and that of the artist's playing, refusing to fully associate or disassociate from either. The resulting dissonance produces a rupture that exposes conservative sexual politics that lingered in the art world after the war.[37]

It may be argued that only with the help of a female collaborator, who adamantly insisted on having her instrument included in their multi-media work, could Paik resolve the infusion of music with sex. The result, however, was not a semi-automatically played 'organi-cord' of a headless woman, but an intersubjective collaboration with a specific and authoritative female performer. In sum, Moorman and Paik challenged artistic conventions and innovatively explored the boundaries between established art forms, the body, and emergent visual technologies. However, the social bias, gender inequality, and patriarchal power structures that considered women as objects of desire for the consuming (male) gaze continued to permeate their work. In contrast to Paik and Moorman's non-critical reflection, Kubota's work directly took up questions of gender, sexuality, and intertwined personal relationships in the power hierarchies of Fluxus networks, and the world more broadly.

VAGINA PAINTING (1964)

Two years before the debut of *Opera Sextronique* in the United States, Kubota performed *Vagina Painting* on 4 July 1965 in New York's Film-Makers' Cinematheque as part of the 'Perpetual Flux Festival', a series of bi-weekly events organized by George Maciunas.[38] The date also marked the first anniversary of Kubota's move to New York,[39] and *Vagina Painting* remained her first and only solo performance. The provocative performance, in which she painted with a brush secured between her legs, was attended by only 'only ten or so people',[40] mostly consisting of Fluxus colleagues and friends.[41] This initial small audience was one reason why it became canonized only decades later, when art historians started to look into pioneering female performance art of the 1960s.[42] Had it not been for Maciunas, who captured the event in what have since become iconic photographs, its legacy would have been even more uncertain.[43]

Revisiting later statements by Kubota, however, I have deduced another crucial reason for its hesitant reception: her own ambivalence about it. Only after Paik's death did she publish the fact that the performance was his idea and that he asked her to keep this a secret. Reinforcing the narrative of conflating romantic and professional desires, her memoir *My Love, Nam June Paik* (*Naŭi Sarang, Paek Namjun*) claims that — after some hesitation — she agreed that 'prudishness and shame' should not prevent an experimental performance. She even felt sorry for Paik, who — as a man — could not perform a piece that he explicitly conceived for women: 'Since it is your wish, I will do it; after all, I am also an artist.'[44] These quotes from the memoir problematically claim her audacious performance as being conditioned by Paik's authorship of the work. Given that the journalist Nam Jeongho is the male co-author of the book, published in Korean in 2010 (and translated into Japanese in 2013) to foster a glorious image of Paik as the 'greatest video artist',[45] it is not surprising that Kubota does not elaborate why Paik wanted his authorship of *Vagina Painting* to be hidden. Ultimately, it remains unclear whether he was aiming to empower his recent lover as an artist-cum-partner in her own right, or, rather, was egotistically

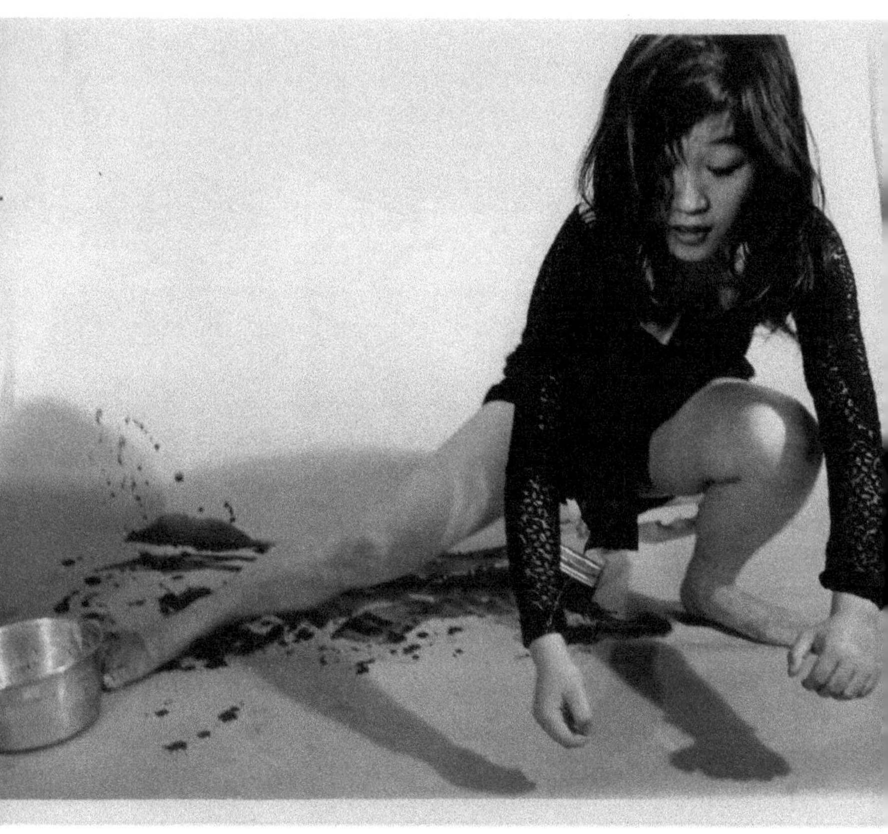

Figure 1. Peter Moore, photograph of a performance of Shigeko
Kubota's *Vagina Painting* (1964), black and white, 20.5 x 15 cm,
print *No. FXC4588* in the archive of Fondazione Bonotto, Colceresa,
Italy. Image courtesy of the Peter Moore Photography Archive,
Charles Deering McCormick Library of Special Collections,
Northwestern University Libraries. © Northwestern University,
Evanston, Illinois, USA.

striving to avoid being accused of instigating situations in which women staged actions that were deemed obscene. In the end, this blind spot in the memoir serves to bolster Paik's authority and remains unchallenged.

Contrary to what the title suggests, *Vagina Painting* was not directly executed with the vagina; rather, Kubota had attached a brush to her underpants (fig. 1). She dipped it in a bucket of red paint and left dynamic traces by repeatedly moving in a squatting position across large rolls of white paper that had been spread out on the floor. While Yoshimoto considers the action 'a parody of the glorified machismo embodied in the actions of male painters', with references to Jackson Pollock's drip paintings executed on canvases laid on the floor, Gutai artist Kazuo Shiraga, who painted with his feet, or Yves Klein's *Anthropometries of the Blue Period* (1960), who used naked women painted blue to 'imprint' bodies onto the canvas, she also acknowledges plausible references to Nam June Paik's *Zen for Head* (1961), a 'calligraphical' line executed with his head leaving a trace of colour on a long stretch of paper.[46] Even if we accept Kubota's claim — published after Yoshimoto's book — that the idea of the performance was actually Paik's, the argument that it critiques grandiose masculine gestures is still valid, since Fluxus artists of both sexes aimed at deconstructing and challenging tropes of singular authorship with their collaborative actions and participatory scores.

The authorship of the idea does not have a significant impact on feminist readings of the work,[47] which focus on who performed it and how. Yoshimoto's analysis sum-

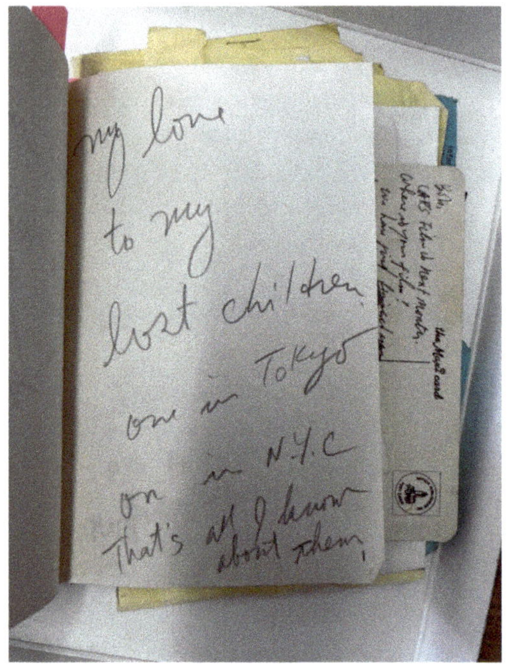

Figure 2. Handwritten note by Kubota, pencil on paper, undated.
Shigeko Kubota Foundation, SKVAF Inventory No.: 19071702, p. 84.
© Estate of Shigeko Kubota/Licensed by VAGA at Artists Rights
Society (ARS), New York.

marizes these findings as stressing the sexist bias of the
male-dominated Fluxus circle, which relegated prolific female participants such as Yoko Ono, Charlotte Moorman,
and Carolee Schneemann to the margins of what was ac-
ceptable within the Fluxus network, as well as to the public.

Kubota's *Vagina Painting* resonates with their work in that she demonstrates the female body as a powerful medium, the literal centre of (human) creation. Choosing red paint instead of black ink diminished the calligraphic associations by alluding to women bleeding during childbirth, as well as throughout their menstrual cycles. A more violent association, which none of the earlier interpretations mention, is that of miscarriage, abortion, or even sexual abuse. Kubota's diaries, which are archived in the Shigeko Kubota Foundation, were examined posthumously and revealed that the artist had perhaps dealt with miscarriage even earlier than her marriage to David Behrmann.[48] In an undated, casually hand-written statement she muses: 'my love | to my | lost children | one in Tokyo | on[e] in N.Y.C. | That's all I know about them' (fig. 2).[49] That said, there are no other materials that might suggest the poetic lament refers to her own personal experience during her early career in Tokyo, before she emigrated to New York. In addition, the existential experience implicitly echoes one of her memoir's anti-climaxes, the day that she describes as her 'sad marriage' to Paik, so that she could benefit from his health insurance to remove her cancerous uterus.[50] Charging her creative painterly traces with allusions to a bleeding vagina may therefore also have been Kubota's way of dealing with personal experiences that also coincidentally foreshadowed an illness that rendered her infertile.

After this powerful debut performance, the fact that the artist neither continued staging *Vagina Painting* nor developed other performances that placed her body centre stage may seem surprising. However, a multitude of reasons were surely enough to discourage her, including Kubota's artistic self-understanding as a sculptor, a general uneasiness with performing on stage,[51] the potential personal significations of this work, the fact that Paik's authorship was involved, and the critical, if not outright negative reactions from the initial audience. That said, it did not prevent Kubota from continuing to engage with gender and body-related issues.

VIDEO POEM (1970–75)

A similarly intimate, but less scandalous work that emphasizes Kubota's take on the female body, her personal relationships, and the process of becoming an independently working (female) video artist is her first video installation, *Video Poem* (1970–75) (fig. 3). Kubota placed a small monitor in a purple nylon bag, allowing the viewer only a glimpse of the screen, which remains only partially visible through a small opening created by a zipper in the bag.[52] Interpreters readily associated the organic shape and flesh-like colour of the bag with a womb and the outline of the opening with a vulva, even a '*vagina dentata* (toothed vagina), a Surrealist metaphor for the male fear of castration', as Yoshimoto has pointed out.[53] Kubota had originally created the bag for her boyfriend Takehisa Kosugi in the context of the 'Yomiuri Independent Exhibition' in Tokyo in 1963, where he used it to perform his *Chamber Music*,

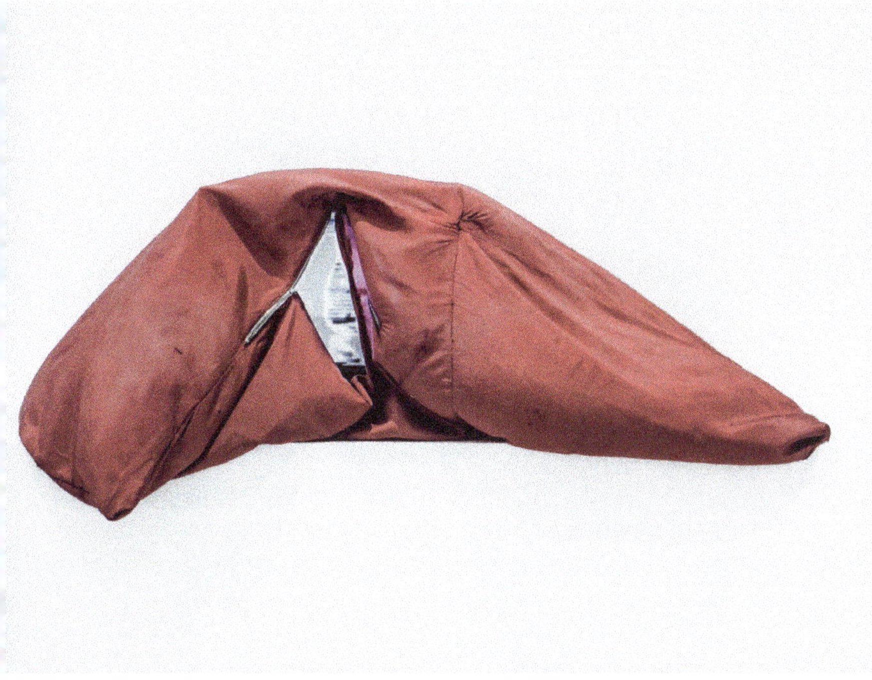

Figure 3. Shigeko Kubota, *Video Poem*, mixed media installation including video (colour) on monitor, electric fan, and zipped textile bag, 1970–75. Installation view from the survey exhibition *The Body Electric* at Walker Art Center (30 March–31 July 2019). Image courtesy of Walker Art Center, Minneapolis, USA. © Estate of Shigeko Kubota/Licensed by VAGA at Artists Rights Society (ARS), New York.

a striptease-like performance that took place inside the bag.[54]

Importantly, Kubota herself associated a typical gendered conflict with the work:

> I used to support him [Kosugi]. I worked three jobs. And I said to him, 'Why don't you work?' and he said 'Because I am a composer.' So I said, 'So where are your compositions?' 'I give you one,' he said, and he gave me this piece, this bag which I inflate with the air from a fan, with wind, like breath, you know.[55]

She wittily refutes Kosugi's ambivalent gift by re-appropriating the bag, inserting herself in it and maintaining the suspense between opening and closing through the half-zipped opening. The latter effectively reinforces the looped movements of the video-synthesized flickering, blurring, and constantly morphing outlines of her head on the screen placed inside the bag. The fan's humming sounds further animate the bag as if it were a breathing being, thus transforming the erotic associations of the striptease that supposedly took place when Kosugi performed inside the bag into the more open signification of Kubota's self-depiction. In sum, the warmly glowing, organically shaped sculpture recalls a womb-like incubator, in which the 'I', Kubota, is nested, re-born as a self-conscious and sensitive being that can be tentatively glimpsed by the audience, but not stripped of her shelter or reductively objectified to specific (female) bodily functions, features, or gestures. Kubota authoritatively portrays herself in a constant state of flux, forever evolving and oscillating between a known being and being known anew. Tying herself intimately to the video apparatus that governs her image in a double sense, she stresses how its (dis-)positional visualizing powers both form and inform pictures of herself as well as the world, thus literally showing how she — a woman — makes a/her world. In addition, she confidently re-appropriates a work created by her former lover, indicating that she has recovered and overcome the gender conflicts characteristic of their (artistic) relationship and perhaps even the trauma of miscarriage. Reusing the bag, but filling it with her own ways of knowing and being in the world, seems quite literally part of the diffractive, intra-actional practice that Barad defines as 'worlding'.[56] The biographical aspects are not forgotten, but become a constitutive part of her first authoritative self-staging in video.[57] Consequently, the work strikes an essential balance between socio-political allusions of being a woman artist, and thus both subject to particular female bodily experiences and power structures in a male dominated art world, and expressions of a sensual and self-empowering artistic subjectivity that transgresses conventional female self-portraits, resulting in a feminist worlding practice.

'VIDEO IS VENGEANCE OF VAGINA'

The text published on Kubota's invitation to the display of *Video Poem* at The Kitchen on 7 June 1975 in New York further radicalizes the poetic aspect of the work. It can be understood as the self-authorizing, gender-conscious motto of her whole oeuvre:

> Man thinks, 'I think, therefore I am.'
> I, a woman, feel, 'I bleed, therefore I am.'
> Recently I bleed in half inch … 3M or SONY … ten
>   thousand feet long every month.
> Man shoots me every night … I can't resist.
> I shoot him back at broad daylight with vidicon or tivicon
>   flaming in over-exposure.
> *Video is Vengeance of Vagina.*
> *Video is Victory of Vagina.*
> *Video is Venereal Disease of Intellectuals.*
> *Video is Vacant Apartment.*
> *Video is Vacation of Art.*
> *Viva Video…* [58]

The introductory five lines contextualize the anaphora 'Video is…' as emerging from a tense male-female relationship. While the author stresses difference in the beginning — men 'think', women 'bleed', i.e. rationality and intellect versus the biological aspect or natural function of the female body — she also reveals a crucial fascination with the opposite sex: 'I can't resist.' This essential attraction turns into a mutual 'shooting (back)', and the poetic 'I' as 'bleed[ing] in half inch' becomes a corporeal metaphor for video as an existential, cyclical, and generative part of life, the medium of a female, even consciously feminist 'worlding' practice.

Ultimately, Kubota's concept of video characterizes it as a sexual medium. Although her concept does not transgress the rationalist notion of a fe-/male binary, but rather stresses difference, it shows the wounding effects that this modern concept can have. In particular, the notions of 'vengeance' and 'victory of vagina' — presumably over its male counterpart — seem to follow the logic of a battle rather than a mutually nurturing relationship, while the ensuing 'venereal disease', 'vacant apartment', and 'vacation of art' evoke continuous ailing, a draining of the relationship, resulting in subjective emptiness. Finally, it sets the 'I' apart from 'art', or at least questions the latter by sending art on 'vacation' in the double sense of distancing it as well as taking time off from it. Consequently, 'video' seems to emerge as a generative medium that thrives on binary gender tensions, acknowledging male and female positions as poles that mutually constitute each other. 'Video' in the double sense of the visual technology and the literal translation of viewing — as in the Latin, 'I see' — is thus poetically framed as being simultaneously both a heightened state of perception, even 'over-exposure' tied to a gendered human condition, and a state of continuous becoming. Kubota's insistence on emotionally charged terms such as 'vengeance' and 'viva' shows that affects are an existential, inseparable part of her worlding through video.

In a later interview, Kubota confirmed that, 'video has allowed both men and women to co-exist in the same space [...] It was equal to both men and women because it was new and fairly inexpensive and we all had the same access to it',[59] adding, 'Male or female, art is art. People can put me in the Feminist category all they want, but I didn't think I can make any real contribution other than my work as an artist.'[60] This statement must be seen in the context of radical second-wave feminism in the United States, which largely accepted essential gender difference and perpetuated whiteness as its blind spot, excluding non-white 'others', which seems to have alienated Kubota. While both *Vagina Painting* and her first video, *Europe in ½ Inch per Day* (1972), demonstrate Kubota's interest in subverting the conventional, heteronormative, white gaze, the works nevertheless still largely adhere to a dichotomous understanding of gender as a male-female binary. However, in her later works, such as the conceptually engaged *Duchampiana* Series (1975–83), as well as her environmentally-inspired works *Three Mountains* (1976–79) and *River* (1979–81),[61] Kubota deployed the more intimate, documentary mode of the 'video diary' in order to develop a more procedural, dynamic, and relational understanding of the complex interactions between humans and nature. Following Paik's stroke in 1996, she revisited the motifs of transience, illness, and death that also characterized some earlier works.[62] Nevertheless, the tense gender relations in *Sexual Healing* (1998) — when viewed retrospectively — now appear wrapped in irony. The footage is realistically rendered without video synthesized modulation and tragicomically limited to the compressed timing of its eponymous song.

SEXUAL HEALING (1998)

With just 4:10 minutes of colour and sound, *Sexual Healing* is Kubota's shortest video work. It documents how Paik tries to recover from stroke-induced hemiplegia supported by several young nurses. The stroke caused a strong caesura in both artists' lives.[63] While Paik was bolstered by artistic assistants and friendships with pioneering curators who allowed him to keep exhibiting, taking care of her husband effectively prevented Kubota from continuing her own artistic work. Consequently, *Sexual Healing* is one of only three videos that she authorized in the two decades before her own death.[64] At first glance, the film appears to be highly ironic, given the decision to set it to the pop song *Sexual Healing* (released in 1982) by the African-American singer Marvin Gaye; the erotic fantasy described in the music is severely compromised by images of a paralysed and visibly aged Paik who can only move his limbs with the help of caretakers. The lyrics' stereotypically male and sexist expectations are counteracted when the camera focuses on the physically demanding labour required from the caretakers, who only grasp the weakened artist to help him stand. However, the lyrics' sexual theme obviously underscores Paik's gestures when he makes abrupt, intrusive, and clearly one-sided advances on the nurses, suddenly kissing one helper on the cheek, smacking her bottom or even head in an uncontrolled movement. These moments raise the spectre of sexual harassment rather than suggesting harmless signs of affection or even gratitude displayed by an otherwise impotent patient. They also radically depart from the collaboratively staged black-and-white series of photographic self-portrayals that the artist couple commissioned in 1974, in which they humorously demonstrate their mutual 'shooting' with film cameras (as invoked earl-

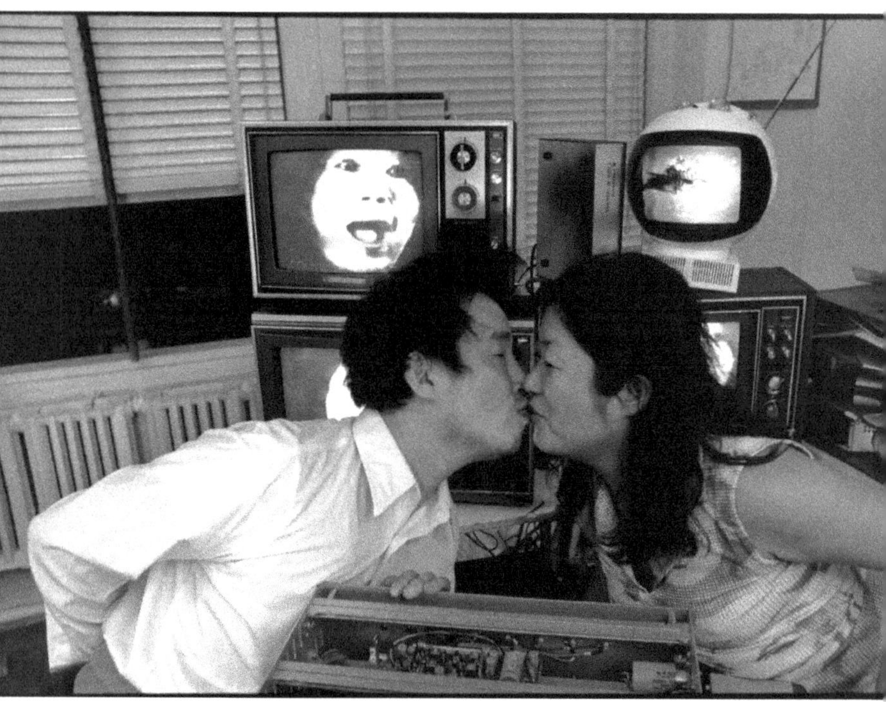

Figure 4. Tom Haar, black-and-white photograph showing Nam June Paik and Shigeko Kubota kissing in their studio loft apartment at Westbeth Artists Housing in New York City, no fixed size from 35 mm negative, 1974. © Tom Haar.

ier in Kubota's poem) and show themselves kissing each other literally at eye level (fig. 4).[65]

Kubota's written explanation frames *Sexual Healing* without irony or critical reflection on the tension between the masculinist lyrics, her ailing but encroaching husband,

and the nurses who are too occupied with stabilizing their patient and probably too precariously situated in the hospital's hierarchy to remonstrate against Paik's invasive actions. This tension is stressed by the fact that it is Kubota's female eye governing the camera, and viewers can only read her account of the situation in the catalogue accompanying her exhibition at Maya Stendhal Gallery in 2007:

> The following morning after Nam June was hospitalized, two healthy and young female therapists took him out of the bed to start his rehabilitation. These single women, who just graduated from college, were wearing red lipstick and tights. They held Nam June like a baby, pressing him hard against their voluptuous breasts [...] They went on asking things like, Are you officially married with your wife? or, Do you have children? If we didn't have children, were they interested in having an affair? I was puzzled [...] They also asked me, You and Mr. Paik are video artists, right? Why don't you bring your camera? Why don't you videotape his walking therapy so he can watch himself? Until then, I was reluctant to take the camera to the hospital, thinking, maybe the other patients would feel intimidated. Encouraged by their suggestion, I shot the video of Nam June engaged in his exercise. I don't want to see it, Nam June said, and refused to watch the video. Perhaps he did not want to confront the reality of what had happened to him. To the melody of Sexual Healing, I made a video work for healing, for Nam June and his therapists.[66]

Kubota's account is striking in at least two respects: on the one hand, she underlines the youth, sex appeal, and perhaps flirtatiousness of the nurses, contrasting it with her own stance as the bewildered wife of a paralysed patient who prosaically documents what her husband has lost in health, mobility, and attraction through the stroke (fig. 5). Since we only have her account, it is unclear whether her depiction of the nurses is accurate or scripted in order to portray the late Paik as more attractive than he actually was in the eyes of the female staff. On the other hand, Kubota acknowledges Paik's discomfort with (watching) the video, which implicitly demonstrates her own, powerful position and independent decision to tape the encounter nonetheless. Ultimately, Kubota suggests the video was a personal-made-public way to visually 'heal' Paik and his therapists. At least implicitly, she also points to the video as being a means to comfort herself about his sickness and to encourage them both to face the situation supported by the care and optimism of others. The work thus demonstrates in a very literal sense how the aging artist-couple depends on others, not just in terms of medical care but also regarding artistic inspiration on Kubota's side, in the sense that she finds a way to continue her video diary work despite being preoccupied with care for her partner. Intergenerational collaboration becomes a necessary condition to carry on with basic physical functions such as standing and walking, as well as shooting videos, while Kubota's verbal silence about what can be viewed as the artist's harassment puts intergenerational understanding and female solidarity into

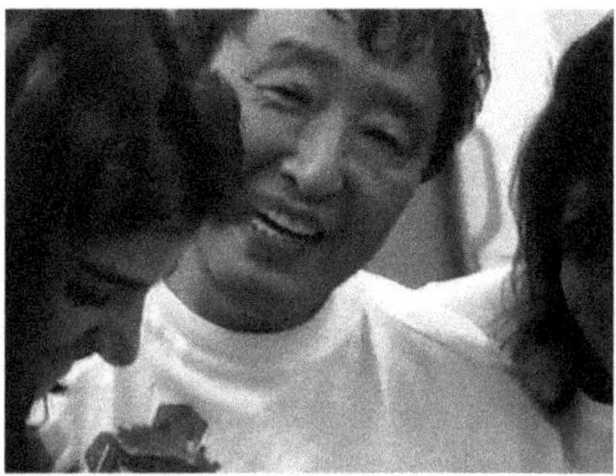

Figure 5. Video still of Shigeko Kubota's *Sexual Healing*, 04:20
minutes, in colour and sound, edited to the eponymous pop song by
Marvin Gaye (1982), edited by Daniel Hartnett, 1998. This scene
occurs for the first time at 00:04 min. and also concludes the film at
04:00 min. Courtesy of Electronic Arts Intermix (EAI), New York.
© Estate of Shigeko Kubota/Licensed by VAGA at Artists Rights
Society (ARS), New York.

question at the same time. Given her acknowledgment of
Paik's unwillingness to view the film, it even begs the question of whether she is abusing her power over the disabled
body of her husband.

It is therefore unsettling to see how Kubota's attention to the facial expressions of the nurses hovers between dwelling on their strenuous working conditions,
gender, and non-white ethnicity[67] — typical of immigrant
women's exploitation in the field of low-paid care work —
and objectifying and capitalizing on their youth and beauty
in the interest of an obviously internalized male gaze that
eerily resonates with the predatory lyrics. The multi-ethnic
constellation of caretakers also points to the boom of fe-

male immigrants working in the growing care economies of aging Western societies. In an uncanny way, Kubota's focus on the caretakers echoes her and Paik's experience of immigration and mirrors her own efforts to take care of her husband as a slightly younger and healthier wife. Ultimately, however, Paik remains the paying patient to whom the rehabilitation facility's employees cater, while Kubota remains the authoritative video eye, who wields the power to film the situation, and steers our perspective. A critical view therefore suggests that her authority as next of kin effectively allowed her to benefit from the nurses' professional performance in two ways: in terms of her husband's physical healing as well as her artistic oeuvre. Therefore, her authoritative position is not to be confused with that of the nurses, despite shared experiences of caretaking, immigration, and gender (fig. 6). Bluntly stated, Paik's unsolicited kisses and slaps were tolerated by women who could probably ill afford to lose their jobs,[68] while Kubota took the ethically questionable liberty of documenting Paik's disabled body, as well as his harassing actions on video and attributing these to 'sexual healing'.

The resulting ambiguity is irresolvable as it can be read in two ways: either as presenting the gaze of a loving but somewhat laconic or disillusioned artist wife who thinks that her husband's erotic desire for his carers might be a sign of his physical recovery, with the nurses' silent endurance of his advances signifying their acceptance, or even — in light of their own youthful erotic energy — encouragement; or it can be read as a subconscious or possibly

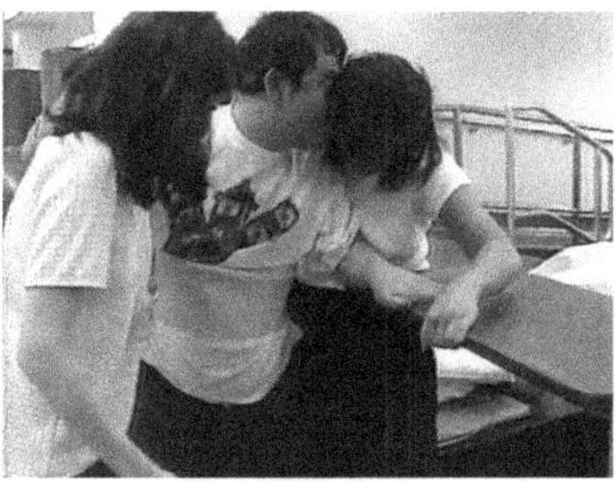

Figure 6. Video still of Shigeko Kubota's *Sexual Healing*, 04:20 minutes, in colour and sound, edited to the eponymous pop song by Marvin Gaye (1982), edited by Daniel Hartnett, 1998. This scene occurs for the first time at 00:11 min. and shows Paik kissing one of his caretakers. Courtesy of Electronic Arts Intermix (EAI), New York. © Estate of Shigeko Kubota/Licensed by VAGA at Artists Rights Society (ARS), New York.

deliberate visual indictment of her husband's extramarital desires and sexual harassment of his carers that works in ironic contrast to her verbal narrative. In the latter view, showcasing the fraught situation with a camera can be read as shock therapy, 'healing' Kubota and the viewer of any naïve assumptions about love and care, especially in long-term relationships and old age, where harmony, mutual understanding, selfless support, and moderated sexual desire free of power and gender struggles do not necessarily prevail.

WHAT KIND OF CARE?

The kind of caretaking that Kubota exhibits here is thus a rather radical, subjective, and one-sided practice, one that does not strive for intergenerational, female, or migrant solidarity, but nevertheless points to these issues as being at stake. As Édith-Anne Pageot has aptly summarized:

> If care can be broadly defined as a relational set of practices and discourses based on attentiveness and a feeling of concern for others, its definition is neither simple nor univocal. Care is not always infused with reciprocity. The discourse of care can be entangled with paternalistic attitudes, empowering those already in a position of power, and thus reinforcing patterns of domination. Care sometimes aligns with victim rhetoric, especially within colonial institutions. *Self-care* can be seen as a narcissistic attitude resulting from late capitalism and of neoliberal ideology of wellness, which promotes productivity, independence, and self-sufficiency. This ideology diminishes individuals who do not fit these constructed categories as being 'precarious bodies', 'dependent' or 'disabled'. [...] But Judith Butler [...] reminds us that 'precarity' is a by-product of neoliberalism based on two principles: competition and inequality.[69]

Given the history of Kubota and Paik competing in the field of emergent video art and the specific gender inequality of their generation, Kubota's ambivalent way of caring about her husband, as well as herself, seems to affectively and radically world a particular 'precarity'. *Sexual Healing* presents Kubota's attempt to capture the thin line between powerful imaging subject and dependent object in the context of neo-liberal and patriarchal social structures.

Going beyond the ethical questions that haunt the video archive in this regard, this work posits itself as a metaphorical 'cure' to, on the one hand, the gendered realities of caretaking and, on the other, patriarchal structures determining the reception of video artists. Since issues of age, sex, and care are rarely addressed together in video works, and moreover, Kubota's film presents the singular case of a female artist documenting the disability of her male artist partner in advanced age, *Sexual Healing* constitutes an absolute rarity that is worth a second look.[70]

The seemingly merciless revelation of Paik's motionless and skinny limbs, which the camera zooms in on several times, juxtaposed with the nurses' concentrated faces, heaving Paik to a standing position, and the artist's own facial expression — oscillating between physical strain and a good humoured smile — all rendered in the guise of a pop music video, shows Kubota's skilful fusion of existential themes and a popular medium. The longer we look, however, the more generally applicable and mundane the situation appears to be in an era of advanced medicine and longer lifespans in Western societies. In contrast to their usual artistic practices, which heavily modified footage using a video synthesizer, Kubota did not modify the images, favouring clear cuts, rapid zooms, no fading, and only occasional tilting of the camera, as if to make sure that the result would not deviate too much from the personal reality that she captured.[71] *Sexual Healing* thus presents us with a reality that is heightened through the 'low tech' repetition of scenes and handheld shooting, counteracting both the avant-garde aesthetic of Paik and Kubota's previous work, as well as the highly polished and technically elaborate aesthetic of deliberately composed music videos.[72]

Comparing *Sexual Healing* with Paik's earlier work, which attempted to fuse sex and music, we can read it as a more radical and critical retake on the issue. Partially following her diaristic mode, Kubota puts her husband centre-stage in a personal situation where he is a helpless, immobile shadow of his former (artistic) self. The fact that he is not in control of his body, except for one arm, turns the lascivious and phallocentric lyrics — alternately calling 'get up, get up, wake up, wake up [...]' and 'Baby, now, let's get down tonight' — into a tragicomedy recalling the long-standing topoi of the ridiculous and lewd old man.[73] This is especially the case when the singer insists, 'I can't hold it much longer, [...] It's getting stronger and stronger', while Paik is obviously not even able to stand up unaided. The male erotic fantasy of 'sexual healing' and the nurse objectified as 'medicine' — which Marvin Gaye conjures with 'You're my medicine, open up and let me in/Darling, you're so great, I can't wait for you to operate' — is thus drastically contrasted with the stoic, non-arousing work performed by the nurses. If anything, the penetrating agent is actually the merciless camera intruding into an unsettling physical situation that renders Paik as object of the (female) gaze and subject to the caretakers' physiotherapeutic labour rather than as an active, powerful agent behind a camera.

Charging the scene with sexual connotations thus requires a lot of imagination and determination on all sides. Describing Kubota's ironic strategy as filming Paik with 'a twinkle in her eye, just as the grand master of Fluxus [Paik] always had' and the result as a 'very beautiful declaration of love' thus only accounts for half the story — if that — and presents an utterly romanticized reading.[74] The other, more complex and disturbing half is indeed better described as the 'vengeance of vagina' taken by the powerful, ambivalent, scrutinizing and at the same time loving camera eye/I of Kubota, who is not afraid of showing the ambiguous figure that her husband has become. Consequently, she 'worlds' our view, introducing the diffractive view of a female artist-cum-wife that enables a feminist intra-action, rather than subscribing to established norms of gender interaction and hierarchies.

Kubota's film zooms in on a nexus of taboos that are rarely addressed collectively in a visual medium: aging bodies, sexual desire, medical care, and love. A few exhibitions, such as *The Art of Aging* in Dresden and Berlin in 2008, have poignantly explored the social taboo of 'sexuality in older age' from a scientific as well as an artistic, self-explorative point of view, noting the commercialization of 'golden agers' in the advertising industry and cinema.[75] However, there were no direct depictions of desiring, erotic, or sexually-active aged bodies, despite many images of (partially) naked older people. Similarly, the more comprehensive survey show *Aging Pride* at the Belvedere Museum in Vienna in 2017 only presented a very few instances of eroticism, as if the very definition of age and aging was the absence of Eros and the waning of sexual activity and desire.[76] Sexually charged images were not avoided because artists feared accusations of pornography, but rather because depictions of age are generally tied to the fact that aging renders bodies (socially) invisible, while beauty and visibility seem to be the exclusive privileges of the young and able.[77]

Kubota's film therefore succinctly inverts iconic art historical tropes of the young, omnipotent male genius amidst his inspiring muses and rather uncannily recalls artful depictions of 'Death and the Maiden(s)' or the male elder lusting after a young female.[78] While *Sexual Healing* only narrowly preceded the increase in motion pictures that featured desire and sexual relationships in advanced age, which began at the end of the 1990s,[79] it differs from their staged nature by self-documenting a private, albeit common reality.[80] Kubota captures her husband's helplessness and disability with candour, including his encroachment on the nurses, but also his resilient, good-humoured way of coping with a physical situation that leaves no hope of a complete recovery. It echoes Susan Sontag's observation that 'Advanced age is undeniably a trial, however stoically it may be endured. It is a shipwreck, no matter with what courage elderly people insist on continuing the voyage. The objective, sacred pain of old age is of another order than the subjective, profane pain of aging'.[81]

However, as Sontag had already stressed by 1972, aging entails a 'double standard' for men and women in modern Western societies, since her beauty is exclusively tied to youth, while men are granted two ideals, the boy as well as the grown man. In contrast to women, the aging bodies of men are accepted in the belief that their skills, wisdom, and power grow over the years.[82] This ambivalence informs Kubota's video. It renders Paik's rehabilitation efforts into an act of courage, facing the stroke, and imagines the nurses as cheerleaders. Suggestively, Kubota herself commands the apparatus that frames the film, but remains largely invisible behind the camera; her own aging becomes the work's blind spot, despite implicitly conditioning our view. Kubota only appears in front of the camera in two short scenes. The first occurs at the beginning of the clip (00:13 min) and shows a close-up of Paik kissing her on the cheek for less than a second. We can read it as an almost hidden moment motivating the film, but also showing Kubota as only one among many, much younger women caring for Paik and receiving his (erotic) attention. The second scene shows her sitting next to him on a bench, patting his belly and giving him a quick kiss (01:13 min) (fig. 7). The flash-like appearance does not give away much about her own aging and condition, but portrays her as an active, caring, and affectionate partner. Consequently, these scenes do little to break the dominance of footage showing her husband being professionally cared for by others and making improper advances. As Paik is not active in returning Kubota's kiss in the second scene, just bending his head a bit without changing his overall posture, the scene underlines Kubota's gesture as a demonstration of self-empowerment that consciously takes into account the fact that they are being filmed, rather than showing a moment of unselfconscious, mutual intimacy. In sum, Kubota ambivalently hints at the framing apparatus without actually giving up the power she wields in the whole *mis-en-scène* as caretaker, as well as camerawoman and film director. It echoes the Vietnamese film director Trinh T. Minh-ha's ethnographical observation that this is a strategy applied by a filmmaker understood as a subject-in-process who allows for a 'reflexive interval'. Defined as a place 'in which the play within the textual frame is a play on this very frame, hence on the borderlines [...], where a positioning within constantly incurs the risk of de-positioning, and where the work, never freed from historical and socio-political contexts nor entirely subjected to them, can only be itself by constantly risking being no-thing'.[83]

NO HAPPY 'HEALING' IN A HETERO-NORMATIVE, ABLE-BODIED WORLD?

Taking the title's promise of 'sexual healing' into critical account, the video openly confronts ailing, disability, the infliction of harm (on the nurses), unrequited (sexual) desire, and the longing of a wife for her husband's former healthy body and acknowledges that healing remains only a matter of gradual improvement. It is not yet tied to a

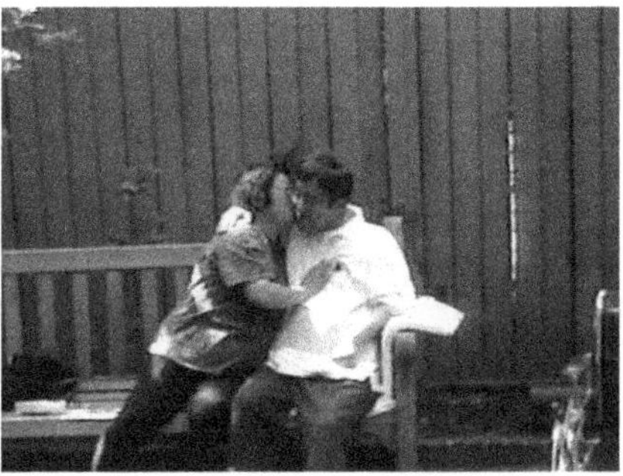

Figure 7. Video still of Shigeko Kubota's *Sexual Healing*, 04:20
minutes, in colour and sound, edited to the eponymous pop song by
Marvin Gaye (1982), edited by Daniel Hartnett, 1998. This scene
occurs only once, at 01:13 min., and shows Kubota kissing Paik on a
bench. Courtesy of Electronic Arts Intermix (EAI), New York.
© Estate of Shigeko Kubota/Licensed by VAGA at Artists Rights
Society (ARS), New York.

more radical queer or crip theoretical critique of the conditions that underscore gendered issues of love, aging, and
care, but seems embedded and emblematic of what Robert
McRuer has described as the normalization of heterosexu-
ality and able-bodiedness characterizing Western (post-)
modern cultures.[84] Following the neo-capitalist paradigm
of flexibility, this particularly produced cinematic representation of more 'flexible' bodies undergoing an identity
crisis related to gender and disability, stereotypically resolved in epiphanies that re-stabilize the heterosexual and
able body as the norm in Hollywood films since the 1990s:
'[Here, t]he flexible subject is successful precisely because
he or she can perform wholeness through each recurring

crisis.'[85] Similarly, Kubota's video seems to suggest that heterosexual desire invigorates (sick) men across the world — on the visual level of the video it's Paik's Asian body, on the resonating level of the pop song's original commercial video it's Gaye's Afro-American body — while the lyrics actually describe sexual desire *as* the sickness itself and can be interpreted more openly as applicable to various sexualities. In contrast to Hollywood's epiphanies, however, Kubota's video refrains from delivering the desired happy 'healing'. Instead, it painfully upholds the double tension of subjecting female bodies to heteronormative male desire as well as actual sexual harassment, while portraying the male body as 'failing', because of age, illness, and — at least in the eyes of feminist viewers — machismo. It thus indirectly reveals the tragic power of heteronormative gender and able-bodied norms that drive Paik's pop-fuelled 'flexible' struggle to manage a crisis, which is ultimately an unmanageable, collective one that also attests to the considerable ethical and artistic 'flexibility' Kubota practises to come to cinematic terms with her position and role in such a compromised world.

The video thus dwells on an essential wound constituted by aging/ailing and underpinned by fixed binary gender norms in ways that do not yet enable 'healing [… as] a movement from possession to relating, from loss to mourning, from reduction to plenitude' as sociologist Rolando Vázquez emphasized when thinking about the social legacies of coloniality and decolonial options.[86] *Sexual Healing* still hovers indecisively between superficially rejecting 'the sensing of the wound' and 'a turn in our dispositions towards the real, from enunciation to listening, from extraction to cultivation, from appropriation to reception', which makes it even more haunting to watch.[87] Yet, it is this ambiguous troubling of video art's archive that renders the work a testament to the fraught issues of artistic authority, collaboration, and canonization when it comes to gender.

Arguably, taking care of the globally acknowledged 'father of video art' required Kubota to perform a very complex and at times painful exercise of self-authorization. When putting him on display in a way that differs from how he is usually shown, or how he wanted to see himself, she empowers and publicly projects her own gaze. Hers is a gaze that is characterized not only by romantic love, but also formed by the life-long experience of being easily overlooked as the woman artist in his shadow. Ultimately, sexual healing therefore means much more than a sexist provocation on the level of the title, an ironic reflection on desire, age, and disability, as well as a reflection of female labour exploitation and sexual harassment in care captured by the filmed reality. If we see the film as another provocative iteration of 'vengeance of vagina', it stresses the central role of affect in worlding and presents a 'personally, intimately situated, and transcultural'[88] way of expressing a wound caused by unresolved gender-related power structures of the art world and society in general. The video seems to attest that '[p]ractices of knowing and being are not isolatable, but rather they are mutually implicated. We do not obtain knowledge by standing outside of the world;

we know because "we" are *of* the world'.[89] It is as if Kubota had known the concluding lines of Sontag's text, where she envisioned women to have another option:

> They [women] can aspire to be wise, not merely nice; to be competent, not merely helpful; to be strong, not merely graceful; to be ambitious for themselves, not merely for themselves in relation to men and children. [...] Women should tell the truth.[90]

Created after Paik's stroke and put on display after his death at the end of Kubota's own life, *Sexual Healing* helps to explain her wise insistence that she and Paik were not collaborators, but 'comrades' in art. Surely, she is not telling 'the' truth, but 'a' truth, when worlding an existential situation with video and intimately capturing her relationship with Paik, as well as gendered power structures, which forced them to go into battle side-by-side rather than co-creating art, while sharing a life.

NOTES

1   Shigeko Kubota in an interview with filmmaker Jeffrey Perkins, cited in Luciana Galliano, *Japan Fluxus* (Lanham, MD: Lexington Books, 2019), p. 50.

2   I would like to thank the EAI archive, particularly Jooyoung Friedman-Buchanan, for making the video accessible for academic research. My insights into Kubota's work have continuously grown thanks to the warm support of Norman Ballard, founding director of the Shigeko Kubota Foundation New York, which I visited for the first time in 2017 supported by a research grant from the Baden-Württemberg Foundation's 'Eliteprogramm für Postdoktorandinnen und Postdoktoranden'. My 'worlded' perspective on *Sexual Healing* opened and matured thanks to critical and generous feedback by my colleagues from the transatlantic research platform 'Worlding Public Cultures: the Arts and Social Innovation' (WPC), particularly Édith-Anne Pageot, Ming Tiampo, and Eva Bentcheva-Webb as well as its BMBF/DLR-funded WPC team at Heidelberg University, no. 01UG2026. I thank my anonymous peer reviewer for very helpful comments and an insightful critique and the staff of ICI Press Berlin for their skilful copyediting. As part of WPC Heidelberg's research, this chapbook also benefitted from the data storage service SDS@hd, supported by the Ministry of Science, Research and the Arts Baden-Württemberg (MWK) and the German Research Foundation (DFG) through grant INST 35/1503-1 FUGG.

3   Shigeko Kubota, 'Chapter One — Meeting with Nam June', faxed electronically-written manuscript, private archive of Nam Jeongho, unpaginated and undated: 'I met Nam June for the first time on the occasion of the concert called the "Sweet 16 Concert" at Sōgetsu Hall in Tokyo, held 3–5 December 1963. This concert was an event in which about 40 young artists participated and I did an event piece as a homage to George Maciunas. Nam June was in the audience for that perform-

ance. I had learned about George and Fluxus from Takehisa Kosugi (of Group Ongaku), Yoko Ono and Toshi Ichiyanagi, Fluxus members, who were living in New York and had come back to Japan for a visit. I, myself, had corresponded with George personally.' The memoir that she later co-authored with Nam Jeongho does not mention this group concert, but makes the direct encounter with Paik after his own solo concert at Sōgetsu Hall on 29 May 1964 the more significant beginning of their acquaintance. The memoir further states that joining the first staging of Karlheinz Stockhausen's *Originale* in New York in September 1964 became their first date and saw them spending the night together in her apartment. Shigeko Kubota and Jeongho Nam, 나의 사랑, 백남준 (*Naŭi Sarang, Paek Nam-jun — My Love, Nam June Paik*) (Seoul: Isun, 2010), pp. 31–33 and 96–97. The memoir has also been translated to Japanese by Sonjun Ko in 2013 appearing as: Shigeko Kubota, Chŏng-ho Nam, and Sonjun Ko, 私の愛、ナムジュンパイク (*Watakushi No Ai, Namujun Paiku — My Love, Nam June Paik*) (Tokyo: Heibonsha 2013).

4 Miwako Tezuka, 'Oral History Interview with Shigeko Kubota, Conducted by Miwako Tezuka, October 11, 2009, at Kubota's Residence in New York City', originally posted on post.at.moma.org, retrieved by the Internet Archive <https://web.archive.org/web/20150926114901/https://post.at.moma.org/content_items/344-interview-with-shigeko-kubota> [accessed 24 March 2023]. Emphasis added.

5 *Merce by Merce by Paik Part Two: Merce and Marcel* (1978) and *Allan 'n' Allen's Complaint* (1982).

6 I examine the different registers of collaboration in the chapter dedicated to Kubota and Paik in my upcoming book.

7 Monica Juneja, '"A Very Civil Idea…": Art History and World-Making — With and Beyond the Nation', *Zeitschrift für Kunstgeschichte*, 81.4 (2018), pp. 461–85 (p. 485).

8 In this volume, 'art history' and 'Art History' are used to different effect. The capitalization of 'Art History' signifies this subject as an institutionalized discipline that has typically favoured a Western-centric narrative. The use of lowercase 'art history' de-thrones any sense of

institutionalized authority in favour of the unruly messiness and lived realities of (art) history, acknowledging the pluralistic and dynamic multitude of threads that comprise any history of art.

9   I do not intend to impose a particular definition of 'love' in this case study, but rather follow the subjective narrative of late Kubota, who frequently frames her relationship with Paik as one of 'love'. While this mostly implies a modern, individualist, romantic notion as coined in Western societies, it seems clear from her interviews as well as the video that the artist was well aware of the patriarchal power structures and social expectations attendant on this concept. In particular, they relegate caretaking responsibilities to women and breadwinning duties to men as a problematic dichotomous labour division within married (family) life, regardless of the ideal of equally loving partners.

10 This is the first in-depth academic text examining the work. The video premiered in New York at the Lance Fung Gallery in 2000 and was also shown in *My Life with Nam June Paik* at the Gallery Maya Stendhal in 2007. While Kubota's first Japanese retrospective *Viva Video! The Art and Life of Shigeko Kubota*, touring from Niigata via Osaka to Tokyo in 2021–22, restaged it, the Museum of Modern Art New York chose not to include it in the contemporaneous retrospective, *Shigeko Kubota — Liquid Reality*.

11 Pheng Cheah, 'Worlding Literature: Living with Tiger Spirits', *Diacritics*, 45.2 (2017), pp. 86–114. Pheng Cheah, 'What Is a World? On World Literature as World-Making Activity', *Daedalus. On Cosmopolitanism*, 137.3 (2008), pp. 26–38. Birgit Mara Kaiser, 'Worlding CompLit: Diffractive Reading with Barad, Glissant and Nancy', *Parallax*, 20.3 (2014), pp. 274–87.

12 Ester Peeren, 'Worlding Popular Culture', in *The Bloomsbury Handbook of World Theory*, ed. by Christian Moraru and Jeffrey R. Di Leo (London: Bloomsbury Academic, 2022), pp. 119–30.

13 Karen Barad, 'Posthumanist Performativity: Toward an Understanding of How Matter Comes to Matter', *Signs: Journal of Women in Culture and Society*, 28.3 (2003), pp. 801–31.

14 Vicki Kirby, *Quantum Anthropologies: Life at Large* (Durham, NC: Duke University Press, 2011).

15 Monica Juneja, '"A Very Civil Idea…"'.

16 Birgit Mara Kaiser, 'Worlding CompLit', p. 3.

17 Monica Juneja, '"A Very Civil Idea…"', p. 466. Transcultural approaches to art history supersede earlier post-colonial concepts suggested by scholars such as Homi K. Bhabha, Gayatri Spivak, and Edward Said, which still focused on binary power relations between subject-object, Orient-Occident, and colonizer-colonized. See for example: Monica Juneja, 'Global Art History and the "Burden of Representation"', in *Global Studies: Mapping the Contemporary*, ed. by Hans Belting et al. (Ostfildern-Ruit: Hatje Cantz Verlag, 2011), pp. 274–97; Monica Juneja, 'Kunstgeschichte und kulturelle Differenz. Eine Einleitung', ed. by Matthias Bruhn, Elke Anna Werner, and Monica Juneja, *Kritische Berichte. Zeitschrift für Kunst- und Kulturwissenschaften*, 40.2 (2012), pp. 6–12; Christian Kravagna, 'Toward a Postcolonial Art History of Contact', *Texte zur Kunst*, Globalism, 91 (September 2013), pp. 110–31; Christian Kravagna, *Transmoderne: Eine Kunstgeschichte des Kontakts* (Berlin: b_books, 2017).

18 Birgit Mara Kaiser, 'Worlding CompLit', p. 251, quoting Karen Barad, 'Posthumanist Performativity', p. 817.

19 For a comparison of how eminent post- and de-colonial thinkers such as Walter D. Mignolo, Paul Gilroy, and Achille Mbembe have coined the concept of epistemic pluriversality describing the option of sharing a world in spite of (colonially impacted) differences, see Ina Kerner, 'Countering the Legacies of Colonial Racism: Delinking and the Renewal of Humanism', in *Postcoloniality — Decoloniality — Black Critique: Joints and Fissures*, ed. by Sabine Broeck and Carsten Junker (Frankfurt a.M.: Campus Verlag, 2014), pp. 145–58 (pp. 155–56).

20 On the importance and profile of Naiqua Gallery, see: Midori Yoshimoto, 'Chapter Six: Self-Exploration in Multimedia: The Experiments of Shigeko Kubota', in *Into Performance: Japanese Women Artists in New York* (New Brunswick, NJ: Rutgers University Press, 2005), pp. 169–93 (p. 173); Reiko Tomii, '"A Test Tube" of New Art: Naiqua and the

Rental Gallery System in 1960s Japan', *Afterall: A Journal of Art, Context and Enquiry*, 47 (2019), pp. 146–61.

21 See analysis of her exhibition by Yoshimoto, 'Chapter Six', pp. 171–74.

22 Shigeko Kubota, 'Sexual Healing', in *Shigeko Kubota: My Life with Nam June Paik*, ed. by Jonas Mekas (New York: Maya Stendhal Gallery, 2007), pp. 67–70 (p. 69).

23 For an interpretation relating the works with early 'happening' instructions by Kubota which entailed sadomasochist allusions like 'pricking' or even 'skinning' your lips before 'kissing a man with a moustache in the audience', see Yoshimoto, 'Chapter Six', p. 173.

24 The Museum of Modern Art and Doryun Chong, *Tokyo 1955–1970* (New York: Museum of Modern Art, 2012); Reiko Tomii, *Radicalism in the Wilderness. International Contemporaneity and 1960s Art in Japan* (Cambridge, MA: The MIT Press, 2016); Galliano, *Japan Fluxus*.

25 Yoshimoto, 'Chapter Six', p. 171.

26 See note 3.

27 Yoko Ono returned from New York to live in Tokyo from 1962 to 1964. She had been married to the vanguard composer Toshi Ichiyanagi from 1956 to 1962 and was an important mediator between the experimental art scenes of New York and Tokyo. Midori Yoshimoto, 'The Message Is the Medium', in *Into Performance: Japanese Women Artists in New York* (New Brunswick, NJ: Rutgers University Press, 2005), pp. 79–114 (p. 84).

28 This was especially true for women who wanted to live as independent artists. While her boyfriend Takehisa Kosugi ultimately decided to stay behind, Kubota and her friend Mieko Shiomi, another woman artist and future Fluxus member, emigrated. Yoshimoto, 'Chapter Six', p. 175.

29 For an illustration and contextualization of Kubota's letter to Maciunas announcing her decision to move and planned arrival in New York, see Midori Yoshimoto, 'Fluxus Nexus: Fluxus in New York and Japan', *post.moma.org*, 2013 <https://post.moma.org/fluxus-nexus-fluxus-in-new-york-and-japan/> [accessed 9 September 2022].

30 See Paik's text on the poster announcing *Opera Sextronique* in New York 1967: Nam June Paik, *Niederschriften eines Kulturnomaden: Aphorismen,*

Briefe, Texte, ed. by Edith Decker (Cologne: DuMont Verlag, 1992), p. 122. The elisions are part of the original text. Music history has earlier records of sex on stage, however it figures as part of the acting rather than in the actions of the musicians, see Joan Rothfuss, *Topless Cellist: The Improbable Life of Charlotte Moorman* (Cambridge, MA: The MIT Press, 2014), p. 88.

31   Rothfuss, *Topless Cellist*, p. 185.

32   Ibid., p. 88. See photographs of the performance in *Nam June Paik*, ed. by John G. Hanhardt (New York: Whitney Museum of American Art, 1982), p. 16.

33   Martha Rosler, 'Video: Shedding the Utopian Moment', in *Illuminated Video: An Essential Guide to Video Art*, ed. by Doug Hall and Sally Jo Fifer (New York: Aperture/BAVC, 1990), pp. 31–50 (p. 45).

34   In 1963, Paik convinced Alison Knowles, the only female Fluxus member at the time, to perform in *Serenade for Alison*. The score asks the performer to strip a series of panties worn atop of each other including a 'blood stained' one, eventually putting panties 'on the wall, [...] to look through them at the audience [..., and] to stuff them into the mouth of a music critic'. However, Knowles only performed it twice, realizing that '[The piece] made me isolate an aspect of myself and present it as if it was especially important. Meaning, the femaleness of my body. [...Emphasizing] the abjectness of woman was not my way'. Rothfuss, *Topless Cellist*, p. 89.

35   Laura Wertheim Joseph, 'Messy Bodies and Frilly Valentines: Charlotte Moorman's "Opera Sextronique"', in *A Fest of Astonishments: Charlotte Moorman and the Avant-Garde, 1960s–1980s* (Evanston, IL: Northwestern University Press, 2016), pp. 41–59 (p. 51). Compare Joan Rothfuss, 'Chapter 16 — The People vs. Charlotte Moorman', *Topless Cellist*, pp. 191–206.

36   The label still holds popular value, so much so that the scholarly, researched, comprehensive biography by Joan Rothfuss reused it as its title: Rothfuss, *Topless Cellist*.

37   Joseph, 'Messy Bodies and Frilly Valentines', pp. 48–49.

38   Yoshimoto, 'Chapter Six', p. 232, note 21: 'The performance was originally scheduled on January 22, 1965, but like events by other artists, Kubota's was rescheduled.' See George Maciunas's poster for *Perpetual Fluxus Festival*, reproduced in *In the Spirit of Fluxus*, ed. by Elizabeth Armstrong and Joan Rothfuss (Minneapolis: Walker Art Center, 1993), p. 168.

39   Nevertheless, it may well have felt significant for a Japanese woman artist to take the American stage for the first time on their National Day in order to enact a decisively female and authority-claiming creative gesture. See Yoshimoto, 'Chapter Six', p. 179.

40   Miwako Tezuka, 'Oral History Interview with Shigeko Kubota', unpaginated. In this interview, Kubota continuously mentions that 'no more than 30 people saw it'.

41   Yoshimoto, 'Chapter Six', p. 179.

42   Yoshimoto stresses Carolee Schneemann's performance *Interior Scroll*, which took place a decade later, being inspired by Kubota's *Vagina Painting*, and cites Kristine Stile as one of the early scholars to evaluate women's contributions to Fluxus in the early 1990s. Yoshimoto, 'Chapter Six', pp. 179–83.

43   See photographs in Yoshimoto, 'Chapter Six', pp. 180–81. Compare with the two photographs by Peter Moore dated 4 November 1964: Fondazione Bonotto, 'FONDAZIONE BONOTTO — Kubota, Shigeko — Vagina Painting' <http://www.fondazionebonotto.org/cn/collection/fluxus/kubotashigeko/9752.html> [accessed 29 June 2020], one of which is Figure 1 in this book.

44   Shigeko Kubota and Jeongho Nam, 나의 사랑, 백남준, p. 103. Compare to the earlier interview, in which she claims that it was Paik and Maciunas who had begged her to perform the piece: Miwako Tezuka, 'Oral History Interview with Shigeko Kubota', unpaginated.

45   Jeongho Nam, '프롤로그 (Prologue)', in 나의 사랑, 백남준 (*Naŭi Sarang, Paek Nam-jun — My Love, Nam June Paik*) (Seoul: Isun, 2010), pp. 16–27 (p. 25).

46   Yoshimoto, 'Chapter Six', p. 179.

47 Yoshimoto, 'Chapter Six', pp. 179–83. Yoshimoto summarizes the pioneering interpretations of art historians Kristin Stiles, Amelia Jones, and Kathy O'Dell.

48 Her marriage with the vanguard composer David Behrman (b. 1937) lasted from 1967 to 1969. Yoshimoto quotes from an interview in which Kubota mentions that carrying the heavy camera equipment might have caused a miscarriage, see Yoshimoto, 'Chapter Six', p. 186, note 39.

49 Addition in squared brackets by the author. The original document is archived by the Shigeko Kubota Foundation, SKVAF Inventory No.: 19071702, p. 84.

50 Shigeko Kubota and Jeongho Nam, 'Chapter 7: 슬픈 결혼식 (Sad Marriage)', in 나의 사랑, 백남준 (*Naŭi Sarang, Paek Nam-jun — My Love, Nam June Paik*), pp. 187–94 (p. 192).

51 Miwako Tezuka, 'Oral History Interview with Shigeko Kubota', unpaginated.

52 Katsue Tomiyama, 'The End of an Odyssey: Shigeko Kubota's Large-Scale Retrospective in New York; an Interview with Shigeko Kubota', in *Shigeko Kubota. Video as a Form of Spiritual Collision with the World* (Milan: Fondazione Mudima, 1994), pp. 9–16 (p. 11).

53 Yoshimoto, 'Chapter Six', p. 190.

54 Ibid.

55 Ingrid Wiegand, 'Video Poems', *Soho Weekly News*, 12 June 1975, n.p. Quoted in Yoshimoto, 'Chapter Six', p. 190.

56 Karen Barad, 'Posthumanist Performativity', p. 803. Barad partially follows Donna Haraway's concept of diffraction in Donna Haraway, 'The Promises of Monsters: A Regenerative Politics for Inappropriate/d Others', in *Cultural Studies*, ed. by Lawrence Grossberg, Cory Nelson, and Paula Treichler (New York: Routledge, 1992), pp. 295–337 (p. 300).

57 The video itself was originally called *Video Portrait* and was her very first video film, created in 1970, as mentioned by Rochelle Slovin, 'Foreword', in *Shigeko Kubota: Video Sculptures*, ed. by Mary Jane Jacob and American Museum of the Moving Image (Seattle: American Museum of the Moving Image/University of Washington Press, 1991), p. 5.

58 The invitation card only cited the last six lines of the poem, see my italics. *Kubota Shigeko: Video Sculptures*, ed. by Felix Zdenek, Toni Stooss, and Ursula Perucchi (Berlin: DAAD Galerie, Museum Folkwang, Kunsthaus Zürich, 1981), p. 42.

59 Phong Bui, 'Shigeko Kubota with Phong Bui', *The Brooklyn Rail*, 2007 <https://brooklynrail.org/2007/09/art/kubota> [accessed 10 August 2020].

60 Ibid., unpaginated.

61 Illustration of these works can be seen in the catalogue *Shigeko Kubota — Liquid Reality*, ed. by Maria Marchenkova (New York: The Museum of Modern Art, 2021).

62 Compare *My Father* (1973–75), *SoHo SoAp/Rain Damage* (1985), and *Korean Grave* (1993).

63 Paik had to stop teaching and travelling across the world, concentrating instead on editing video works. In addition, he created little graphic series and painted on the surfaces of TV sets. John G. Hanhardt, 'Nam June Paik: The Late Style (1996–2006)', *Ran Dian* (blog), 17 September 2015 <http://www.randian-online.com/np_announcement/nam-june-paik-the-late-style-1996-2006-grasp-the-eternity/> [accessed 9 September 2022].

64 The nurse Herodine Pluviose shot the scenes of the last video that Kubota published, *Winter in Miami* (2006), featuring the couple together in Miami Beach shortly before Paik's death. It marks the official end of Kubota wielding the camera. Like *Sexual Healing* and *April is the Cruelest Month* (1999), *Winter in Miami* was also edited by Daniel Hartnett. I was unable to get in contact with him to ask him about the editing process.

65 In correspondence with the author, Tom Haar stated that 'I photographed both of them together in 1974, when I was also living in the same Westbeth Artists Housing in lower New York, …. I knew them both from earlier times, starting with when I took some photographs of Paik when he had a solo exhibit at Galeria Bonino in 1971'. He further clarified that the photograph belongs to a series 'requested for promotional (publicity) use' by the artists and that he cannot remember if the kissing was spontaneous, 'but it is more likely that I suggested such a

situation at the conclusion of the photo session'. Tom Haar, two unpublished emails to Franziska Koch, 22 and 23 November 2022.

66 Shigeko Kubota, 'Sexual Healing', p. 67.

67 I was unable to find out in which facility the video was shot or any details of the featured staff, but I believe Paik was being treated either in New York or Miami at the time. Many of the nurses — the overwhelming majority of whom are women — as well as the one male caretaker could all potentially be identified as People of Colour.

68 It remains unclear whether being filmed by his wife increased the pressure on the caretakers to make no apparent objection to Paik's behaviour.

69 Édith-Anne Pageot, 'Connecting Local Communities through Relational Ethics of Care. The Work of Sonia Robertson', *Arte Contexto* (blog), 2021 <https://artcontexto.com.br/portfolio/edith-anne-pageot/> [accessed 9 September 2022], unpaginated. Pageot refers to discussions of disability by Feder Kittay and Richard Sandell in this passage. Also compare the 'universal' call for establishing care as a new social paradigm, which seems chiefly informed by experiences of Western democratic and capitalist countries: Andreas Chatzidakis et al., *The Care Manifesto: The Politics of Interdependence* (London: Verso, 2020).

70 For a brief bibliographical review of English-language writing on the topic as it relates to contemporary art, see Rachel Middleman, 'Aging and Feminist Art: Joan Semmel's Visible Bodies', in *Women, Aging, and Art: A Crosscultural Anthology*, ed. by Frima Fox Hofrichter and Midori Yoshimoto (New York: Bloomsbury Academic & Professional, 2021), pp. 167–81 (p. 168 and note 4, pp. 179–80).

71 *Sexual Healing*, 01:38 and 03:15 min.

72 The official video of Gaye's song features him on stage with four female background singers of different ethnic types, ranging from black via brown to white, scenes in a doctor's room with a lascivious brown-haired nurse administering a 'midnight love potion' and kisses to the singer, and scenes of the two of them driving away in a luxury limousine. It is thus very conventional compared to aesthetically more innovative music videos of the time.

73 For an in-depth examination of these topoi in European art history, see
Sabine Kampmann, 'Ungleiche Paare — Bilder lächerlicher Liebe und
die Verhöhnung geiler Greise — Lucas Cranach, Andres Serrano', in
Bilder des Alterns. Greise Körper in Kunst und Visueller Kultur (Berlin:
Dietrich Reimer Verlag, 2020), pp. 102–11.

74 See transmediale e.V., 'Archive: Sexual Healing', *transmediale/archive*,
1999 <https://transmediale.de/content/sexual-healing> [accessed 4
August 2020], unpaginated.

75 Jana Sylvester and Beate Schultz-Zehden, 'Sexualität im Alter – ein
gesellschaftliches Tabu? Interview mit Beate Schultz-Zehden', in *Die
Kunst des Alterns. Katalog zu den Ausstellungen: Wir sind immer für Euch
da. Über das Versprechen der Generationen*, ed. by Neue Gesellschaft
für Bildende Kunst, Kunsthaus Dresden, Städtische Galerie für Gegenwartskunst, and Cordelia Marten (Berlin: NGBK, 2008), pp. 128–34;
Silvia Bovenschen, 'Runzelsex (so darf man das nicht nennen!)', in
ibid., pp. 126–27; Gabriele Schor, 'Sex, Sensuality, Eroticism in Old
Age: The Feminist Avant-Garde Tackles a Taboo', in *Die Kraft des Alters.
Aging Pride*, ed. by Stella Rollig and Sabine Fellner (Vienna: Verlag
für Moderne Kunst, 2017), pp. 295–320; Thomas Küpper, 'Filmreif.
Altersdarstellungen im Kino', in *Die Kunst des Alterns*, ed. by Neue Gesellschaft für Bildende Kunst, et al., pp. 100–07.

76 See *Die Kraft des Alters. Aging Pride*, ed. by Rollig and Fellner. The exhibition featured the small and aged, but lasciviously posing Vivienne
Westwood as a reclining nude à la Jacques-Louis David with a young
lover photographed by Annie Leibovitz (p. 247) and photographs by
Juergen Teller, with whom Westwood restages iconic depictions by
François Boucher and Gustave Courbet (pp. 232–33). Aleah Chapin's
oil painting *The Last Droplets of the Day* (2014, p. 227) depicts a cluster
of joyfully hugging and laughing silver-haired naked women *en plein
air*, while Alfred Hrdlicka's graphic *Muss Pornografie schön sein?* (1973,
p. 18) renders an older couple's intercourse as caricature. Only Heidi
Harsieber's photographs *The Beatles* (2001) and *Rapid Fan* (2001, pp.
20–21), from a series in which she captured artist couples in sexual interaction, come close to the topic and documentary intensity of Kubota's
Sexual Healing.

77 Beate Hofstadler, 'Blood, Sweat, and Years: The Disappearance of the Old', in *Die Kraft des Alters. Aging Pride*, ed. by Rollig and Fellner, pp. 187–219.

78 Art historical research on the nexus of age, love, sex, and care yields only few exhibitions and monographs. For a recent recapitulation, see Frima Fox Hofrichter and Midori Yoshimoto, 'Introduction', in *Women, Aging, and Art: A Cross-Cultural Anthology*, ed. by Frima Fox Hofrichter and Midori Yoshimoto (New York: Bloomsbury Visual Arts, 2021), pp. 1–15. Besides the exhibition *Die Kraft des Alters. Aging Pride*, they only mention the show *Old Mistresses: Women Artists of the Past* at the Walters Art Gallery in 1972. In 2008, there was a travelling exhibition presented in Berlin at the nGbK under the title *Ein Leben lang*, and at Kunsthaus Dresden as *Wir sind immer für euch da*, however, before this, only one other show in Germany covered occidental sculpture's engagement with age from antiquity to modernity: *Altersbildnisse in der abendländischen Skulptur*, ed. by Christoph Brockhaus (Duisburg: Wilhelm Lehmbruck Museum, 1998). For a comprehensive cultural history, albeit limited to the West, see *A History of Old Age*, ed. by Pat Thane (Los Angeles: J. Paul Getty Museum, 2005).

79 Heike Hartung, 'Age and Gender in Cultural Discourse: The Double Standard in the Narratives and Images of Aging', in *Die Kraft des Alters. Aging Pride*, ed. by Rollig and Fellner, pp. 257–73 (p. 259).

80 While building on Michel Foucault and Judith Butler, Hartung nevertheless stresses that 'The natural and biological constitution of the aged body cannot be completely subsumed under a performative and culturalist notion of identity'. Ibid., p. 257.

81 Susan Sontag, 'The Double Standard of Aging', in *Essays of the 1960s & 70s*, ed. by David Rieff (New York: Library of America, 2013), pp. 745–68 (p. 746).

82 Ibid., p. 747. See also Hartung, 'Age and Gender in Cultural Discourse', p. 267.

83 Trinh T. Minh-ha, 'Documentary Is/Not a Name', *October*, 52 (1990), p. 96.

84 Robert McRuer and Michael Bérubé, *Crip Theory: Cultural Signs of Queerness and Disability*, Cultural Front (New York: New York University Press, 2006), pp. 30–31.

85 Ibid., p. 17.

86 Rolando Vázquez, *Vistas of Modernity: Decolonial Aesthesis and the End of the Contemporary*, Essay/Mondriaan Fund, 014 (Amsterdam: Mondriaan Fund, 2020), p. 119.

87 Ibid.

88 Monica Juneja, "'A Very Civil Idea...'", p. 310.

89 Karen Barad, 'Posthumanist Performativity', p. 829, quoted from Birgit Mara Kaiser, 'Worlding CompLit', p. 249.

90 Sontag, 'The Double Standard of Aging', p. 768.

REFERENCES

Armstrong, Elizabeth, and Joan Rothfuss, eds, *In the Spirit of Fluxus* (Minneapolis: Walker Art Center, 1993)

Barad, Karen, 'Posthumanist Performativity: Toward an Understanding of How Matter Comes to Matter', *Signs: Journal of Women in Culture and Society*, 28.3 (2003), pp. 801–31 <https://doi.org/10.1086/345321>

Bovenschen, Silvia, 'Runzelsex (so darf man das nicht nennen!)', in *Die Kunst des Alterns*, ed. by Neue Gesellschaft für Bildende Kunst, et al. (Berlin: NGBK, 2008), pp. 126–27

Brockhaus, Christoph, *Altersbildnisse in der abendländischen Skulptur* (Duisburg: Wilhelm Lehmbruck Museum, 1998)

Bui, Phong, 'Shigeko Kubota with Phong Bui', *The Brooklyn Rail*, 2007 <https://brooklynrail.org/2007/09/art/kubota> [accessed 10 August 2020]

Chatzidakis, Andreas, et al., eds, *The Care Manifesto: The Politics of Interdependence* (London: Verso, 2020)

Cheah, Pheng, 'What Is a World? On World Literature as World-Making Activity', *Daedalus: On Cosmopolitanism*, 137.3 (2008), pp. 26–38 <https://doi.org/10.1162/daed.2008.137.3.26>

—— 'Worlding Literature: Living with Tiger Spirits', *Diacritics*, 45.2 (2017), pp. 86–114 <https://doi.org/10.1353/dia.2017.0008>

Fondazione Bonotto, 'FONDAZIONE BONOTTO — Kubota, Shigeko — Vagina Painting' <http://www.fondazionebonotto.org/cn/collection/fluxus/kubotashigeko/9752.html> [accessed 24 March 2023]

Galliano, Luciana, *Japan Fluxus* (Lanham, MD: Lexington Books, 2019)

Hamada, Mayumi, Mihoko Nishikawa, Azusa Hashimoto, Midori Yoshimoto, and Yui Yoshizumi, *Viva Video! The Art and Life of Shigeko Kubota* (Tokyo: Kawade Shobo Shinsha, 2021)

Hanhardt, John G., ed., *Nam June Paik* (New York: Whitney Museum of American Art, 1982)

—— 'Nam June Paik: The Late Style (1996–2006)', *Ran Dian* (blog), 17 September 2015 <http://www.randian-online.com/np_announcement/nam-june-paik-the-late-style-1996-2006-grasp-the-eternity/> [accessed 9 September 2022]

Haraway, Donna, 'The Promises of Monsters: A Regenerative Politics for Inappropriate/d Others', in *Cultural Studies*, ed. by Lawrence Grossberg, Cory Nelson, and Paula Treichler (New York: Routledge, 1992), pp. 295–337

Hartung, Heike, 'Age and Gender in Cultural Discourse: The Double Standard in the Narratives and Images of Aging', in *Die Kraft des Alters. Aging Pride*, ed. by Rollig and Fellner, pp. 257–73

Hofrichter, Frima Fox, and Midori Yoshimoto, 'Introduction', in *Women, Aging, and Art. A Cross-Cultural Anthology*, ed. by Frima Fox Hofrichter and Midori Yoshimoto (New York: Bloomsbury Visual Arts, 2021), pp. 1–15 <https://doi.org/10.5040/9781501349430.0007>

Hofstadler, Beate, 'Blood, Sweat, and Years. The Disappearance of the Old', in *Die Kraft des Alters. Aging Pride*, ed. by Stella Rollig and Sabine Fellner Fellner (Vienna: Verlag für Moderne Kunst, 2017), pp. 187–219

Jacob, Mary Jane, and American Museum of the Moving Image, eds, *Shigeko Kubota: Video Sculptures* (Seattle: American Museum of the Moving Image/University of Washington Press, 1991)

Joseph, Laura Wertheim, 'Messy Bodies and Frilly Valentines: Charlotte Moorman's "Opera Sextronique"', in *A Fest of Astonishments: Charlotte Moorman and the Avant-Garde,*

1960s–1980s (Evanston, IL: Northwestern University Press, 2016), pp. 41–59

Juneja, Monica, 'Global Art History and the "Burden of Representation"', in *Global Studies: Mapping the Contemporary*, ed. by Hans Belting et al. (Ostfildern-Ruit: Hatje Cantz Verlag, 2011), pp. 274–97

—— 'Kunstgeschichte und kulturelle Differenz. Eine Einleitung', ed. by Matthias Bruhn, Elke Anna Werner, and Monica Juneja, *Kritische Berichte. Zeitschrift für Kunst- und Kulturwissenschaften*, 40.2 (2012), pp. 6–12

—— '"A Very Civil Idea…": Art History and World-Making — With and Beyond the Nation', *Zeitschrift für Kunstgeschichte*, 81.4 (2018), pp. 461–85 <https://doi.org/10.1515/ZKG-2018-0036>

Kaiser, Birgit Mara, 'Worlding CompLit: Diffractive Reading with Barad, Glissant and Nancy', *Parallax*, 20.3 (2014), pp. 274–87 <https://doi.org/10.1080/13534645.2014.927634>

Kampmann, Sabine, 'Ungleiche Paare — Bilder lächerlicher Liebe und die Verhöhnung geiler Greise — Lucas Cranach, Andres Serrano', in *Bilder des Alterns. Greise Körper in Kunst und Visueller Kultur* (Berlin: Dietrich Reimer Verlag, 2020), pp. 102–11 <https://doi.org/10.5771/9783496030232>

Kerner, Ina, 'Countering the Legacies of Colonial Racism: Delinking and the Renewal of Humanism', in *Postcoloniality — Decoloniality — Black Critique: Joints and Fissures*, ed. by Sabine Broeck and Carsten Junker (Frankfurt a.M.: Campus Verlag, 2014), pp. 145–58

Kirby, Vicki, *Quantum Anthropologies. Life at Large* (Durham, NC and London: Duke University Press, 2011) <https://doi.org/10.1515/9780822394440>

Kravagna, Christian, 'Toward a Postcolonial Art History of Contact', *Texte zur Kunst, Globalism*, 91 (September 2013), pp. 110–31

—— *Transmoderne: Eine Kunstgeschichte des Kontakts* (Berlin: b_books, 2017)

Kubota, Shigeko, 'Chapter One — Meeting with Nam June', faxed electronically-written manuscript, private archive of Nam Jeongho, unpaginated and undated

—— 'Sexual Healing', in *Shigeko Kubota: My Life with Nam June Paik*, ed. by Jonas Mekas (New York: Maya Stendhal Gallery, 2007), pp. 67–70

Kubota, Shigeko, and Jeongho Nam, 나의 사랑, 백남준 (*Naŭi Sarang, Paek Nam-jun — My Love, Nam June Paik*) (Seoul: Isun, 2010)

Kubota, Shigeko, Chŏng-ho Nam, and Sonjun Ko, 私 の 愛、ナムジュン パイク (*Watakushi No Ai, Namujun Paiku — My Love, Nam June Paik*) (Tokyo: Heibonsha 2013) (Tokyo: Heibonsha 2013)

Küpper, Thomas, 'Filmreif. Altersdarstellungen im Kino', in *Die Kunst des Alterns*, ed. by Neue Gesellschaft für Bildende Kunst, et al. (Berlin: NGBK, 2008), pp. 100–07

Marchenkova, Maria, ed., *Shigeko Kubota — Liquid Reality* (New York: The Museum of Modern Art, 2021)

McRuer, Robert, and Michael Bérubé, *Crip Theory: Cultural Signs of Queerness and Disability*, Cultural Front (New York: New York University Press, 2006)

Mekas, Jonas, ed., *Shigeko Kubota: My Life with Nam June Paik* (New York: Maya Stendhal Gallery, 2007)

Middleman, Rachel, 'Aging and Feminist Art: Joan Semmel's Visible Bodies', in *Women, Aging, and Art: A Crosscultural Anthology*, ed. by Frima Fox Hofrichter and Midori Yoshimoto (New York: Bloomsbury Academic & Professional, 2021), pp. 167–81 <https://doi.org/10.5040/9781501349430.0018>

Minh-ha, Trinh T., 'Documentary Is/Not a Name', *October*, 52 (1990) <https://doi.org/10.2307/778886>

Museum of Modern Art and Doryun Chong, *Tokyo 1955–1970* (New York: Museum of Modern Art, 2012)

Nam, Jeongho, '프롤로그 (Prologue)', in 나의 사랑, 백남준 (*Naŭi Sarang, Paek Nam-jun — My Love, Nam June Paik*) (Seoul: Isun, 2010), pp. 16–27

Neue Gesellschaft für Bildende Kunst, Kunsthaus Dresden, Städtische Galerie für Gegenwartskunst, and Cordelia Marten, eds, *Die Kunst des Alterns. Katalog zu den Ausstellungen: Wir sind immer für Euch da. Über das Versprechen der Generationen* (Berlin: NGBK, 2008)

Pageot, Édith-Anne, 'Connecting Local Communities through Relational Ethics of Care. The Work of Sonia Robertson', *Arte Contexto* (blog), 2021 <https://artcontexto.com.br/portfolio/edith-anne-pageot/> [accessed 9 September 2022], unpaginated

Paik, Nam June, *Niederschriften eines Kulturnomaden: Aphorismen, Briefe, Texte*, ed. by Edith Decker (Cologne: DuMont Verlag, 1992)

Peeren, Ester, 'Worlding Popular Culture', in *The Bloomsbury Handbook of World Theory*, ed. by Christian Moraru and Jeffrey R. Di Leo (London: Bloomsbury Academic, 2022), pp. 119–30 <https://doi.org/10.5040/9781501361975.ch-007>

Rollig, Stella, and Sabine Fellner, eds, *Die Kraft des Alters. Aging Pride* (Vienna: Verlag für Moderne Kunst, 2017)

Rosler, Martha, 'Video: Shedding the Utopian Moment', in *Illuminated Video: An Essential Guide to Video Art*, ed. by Doug Hall and Sally Jo Fifer (New York: Aperture/BAVC, 1990), pp. 31–50

Rothfuss, Joan, *Topless Cellist: The Improbable Life of Charlotte Moorman* (Cambridge, MA: The MIT Press, 2014)

Schor, Gabriele, 'Sex, Sensuality, Eroticism in Old Age: The Feminist Avant-Garde Tackles a Taboo', in *Die Kraft des Alters. Aging Pride*, ed. by Stella Rollig and Sabine Fellner (Vienna: Verlag für Moderne Kunst, 2017), pp. 295–320

Slovin, Rochelle, 'Foreword', in *Shigeko Kubota: Video Sculptures*, ed. by Mary Jane Jacob and American Museum of the

Moving Image (Seattle: American Museum of the Moving Image/University of Washington Press, 1991), p. 5

Sontag, Susan, 'The Double Standard of Aging', in *Essays of the 1960s & 70s*, ed. by David Rieff (New York: Library of America, 2013), pp. 745–68

Sylvester, Jana, and Beate Schultz-Zehden, 'Sexualität im Alter – ein gesellschaftliches Tabu? Interview mit Beate Schultz-Zehden', in *Die Kunst des Alterns*, ed. by Neue Gesellschaft für Bildende Kunst, et al. (Berlin: NGBK, 2008), pp. 128–34

Tezuka, Miwako, 'Oral History Interview with Shigeko Kubota, Conducted by Miwako Tezuka, *October 11*, 2009, at Kubota's Residence in New York City', originally posted on post.at.moma.org, retrieved by the Internet Archive <https://web.archive.org/web/20150926114901/https://post.at.moma.org/content_items/344-interview-with-shigeko-kubota> [accessed 24 March 2023]

Thane, Pat, ed., *A History of Old Age* (Los Angeles: J. Paul Getty Museum, 2005)

Tomii, Reiko, *Radicalism in the Wilderness. International Contemporaneity and 1960s Art in Japan* (Cambridge, MA: The MIT Press, 2016)

—— '"A Test Tube" of New Art: Naiqua and the Rental Gallery System in 1960s Japan', *Afterall: A Journal of Art, Context and Enquiry*, 47 (2019), pp. 146–61 <https://doi.org/10.1086/704206>

Tomiyama, Katsue, 'The End of an Odyssey: Shigeko Kubota's Large-Scale Retrospective in New York; An Interview with Shigeko Kubota', in *Shigeko Kubota. Video as a Form of Spiritual Collision with the World* (Milan: Fondazione Mudima, 1994), pp. 9–16

transmediale e.V., 'Archive: Sexual Healing', *transmediale/archive*, 1999 <https://transmediale.de/content/sexual-healing> [accessed 4 August 2020], unpaginated

Vázquez, Rolando, *Vistas of Modernity: Decolonial Aesthesis and the End of the Contemporary*, Essay/Mondriaan Fund, 014 (Amsterdam: Mondriaan Fund, 2020)

Walters Art Gallery, Ann Gabhart, and Elizabeth Broun, eds, *Old Mistresses: Women Artists of the Past* (Baltimore: Walters Art Gallery, 1972)

Yoshimoto, Midori, 'Fluxus Nexus: Fluxus in New York and Japan', *post.moma.org*, 2013 <https://post.moma.org/fluxus-nexus-fluxus-in-new-york-and-japan/> [accessed 9 September 2022]

—— *Into Performance: Japanese Women Artists in New York* (New Brunswick, NJ: Rutgers University Press, 2005)

Zdenek, Felix, Toni Stooss, and Ursula Perucchi, eds, *Kubota Shigeko: Video Sculptures* (Berlin: DAAD Galerie, Museum Folkwang, Kunsthaus Zürich, 1981)

Worlding Public Cultures

Series Editor
>Ming Tiampo

Managing Editor
>Eva Bentcheva

Assistant Managing Editor
>Kelley Tialiou

Copy Editor
>Francesca Simkin

Editorial Board
>Eva Bentcheva
>May Chew
>Chiara de Cesari
>Birgit Hopfener
>Paul Goodwin
>Alice Ming Wai Jim
>Monica Juneja
>Franziska Koch
>Wayne Modest
>Miriam Oesterreich
>Édith-Anne Pageot
>Ming Tiampo
>Maribel Hildago Urbaneja
>Toshio Watanabe

The publication series takes as its starting point 'Worlding Public Cultures: The Arts and Social Innovation' (WPC), a collaborative research project and transnational platform conceived by the Transnational and Transcultural Arts and Culture Exchange (TrACE) network in 2018.

WPC is funded by the Trans-Atlantic Platform for the Social Sciences and Humanities (T-AP) through a collaboration between the following granting agencies:

> Dutch Research Council (NWO), Netherlands
> Economic and Social Research Council (ESRC), UK
> Federal Ministry of Education and Research (BMBF)/ DLR Project Management Agency, Germany
> Fonds de recherche du Québec — Société et culture (FRQSC), Canada
> Social Sciences and Humanities Research Council (SSHRC), Canada

The WPC publication series is produced through the generous funding of ICI Berlin Institute for Cultural Inquiry, BMBF, NWO, FRQSC, SSHRC, and the National Museum of World Cultures, Netherlands.

REGISTERS IN THE SERIES
Troubling Public Cultures: Case Studies
These single and collaboratively-authored Case Studies explore 'worlding' in different regional, temporal, thematic, institutional, and practice-related contexts.

Worlding Concepts
Worlding Concepts serves as a lexicon of key terminology discussed and developed throughout the WPC project.

Academies
These edited volumes present contributions and discussions from WPC academies and assemblies.

Companions for Thinking and Doing
Companions distil the theoretical insights of the WPC project to provide practice-based reflections, proposals, and questions.

List of published titles at: https://doi.org/10.25620/wpc-print.

www.ingramcontent.com/pod-product-compliance
Lightning Source LLC
LaVergne TN
LVHW051124180726
843512LV00012B/927